The Kris Study Group of the
New York Psychoanalytic Institute

Monograph V

The Kris Study Group of the
New York Psychoanalytic Institute

Monograph V

Trauma

—

Symbolism

Edited by HERBERT F. WALDHORN, M.D.
and BERNARD D. FINE, M.D.

INTERNATIONAL UNIVERSITIES PRESS, INC.
NEW YORK   NEW YORK

LIBRARY OF CONGRESS CATALOGING IN PUBLICATION DATA
Main entry under title:
TRAUMA. SYMBOLISM.

(Kris Study Group of the New York Psychoanalytic
Institute. Monograph 5)
Includes bibliographies.
1. Symbolism (Psychology) 2. Psychic
trauma. I. Waldhorn, Herbert F., ed. II. Fine,
Bernard D., ed. III. Title: Symbolism.
IV. Series: New York. Psychoanalytic Institute.
Ernst Kris Study Group. [DNLM: 1. Psychoanalytic
theory. 2. Symbolism. WI NE802F v. 5 1974 / WM460
T777 1974]

BF173.A2N4313 no. 5 [BF458] 150'.19'508s 150'.19'5
ISBN 0-8236-6643-3   73-6942

Manufactured in the United States of America

FOREWORD

This volume of the Monograph series continues the format of presenting the reports of two different Sections of the Kris Study Group, each of which had devoted a year to the consideration of its topic. Both the study of the subject of Trauma, undertaken by the Group led by Dr. David Beres, and the survey of the subject of Symbolism, under the leadership of Dr. Charles Brenner, reflected the desire to bring some clarification to an area of psychoanalytic theory where the literature was sparse, diffuse, or contradictory. Characteristically, the method of investigation was based on clinical material drawn from the combined experience of the many members of the Group, and on contributions from other sources as well. After studying the relevant literature and the monthly protocols of case histories and clinical and theoretical expositions offered by individual members or small subcommittees, the entire Section hammered out new understandings in wide-ranging and spirited discussions. Summaries of these group discussions were prepared regularly for review and critical explication, and final reports were presented before Plenary meetings of the entire Kris Study Group.

In this volume, two approaches to the presentation of a report of the work of a Kris Study Group can be distinguished. Dr. Donadeo's Monograph attempts to summarize the course and development of the Group's activity and its elaboration of the position of some individual contributions, including the valuable interdisciplinary excursions into the fields of linguistics and anthropology. While only a verbatim transcript could faithfully convey the rich and creative interaction among the many participants, the greater number of whom are not specifically identified by name, the Monograph manages to indicate the mutual influences which led to the viewpoints and conclusions reached at the end of the year.

Dr. Milrod recast the material his Section accumulated in its year's work, presenting it so that it reflected his personal view of the over-all significance and nature of the Group's refinement of the concepts under study. Making use of the clinical data and the other presentations reviewed in the monthly meetings, he organized and ordered them in a way congenial to his own developing understanding of the topic. This acknowledged introduction of a personal emphasis may well provide a valuable reference point for the reader's appreciation of this unique Group creation.

THE EDITORS

CONTENTS

TRAUMA

DAVID MILROD, M.D., *Reporter*

Participants: Drs. David Beres (Chairman)—Theodore Cherbuliez—Jerome Ennis—Bernard D. Fine—Gilbert W. Kliman—Nauttam J. Kothari—Edgar L. Lipton—David Milrod—Joshua M. Perman—Herman Roiphe—Robert J. Sayer.

The concept of psychic trauma holds a central place in psychoanalysis today, clinically and theoretically, just as it did for Freud throughout the entire span of his psychoanalytic work. In the early 1890's it appeared as a legacy from Charcot, with whom he had worked earlier in Paris, but it weaves through all of his writings to his last works in 1939, always important in the understanding of neuroses and, like his other theoretical constructions, always undergoing refinement and expansion.

This fundamental psychoanalytic concept of psychic trauma became the subject of a two-year study by a section of the Kris Study Group of The New York Psychoanalytic Institute led by Dr. David Beres. The ubiquitous nature of psychic trauma made for the ready availability of clinical material and for a wide-ranging and loosely discursive type of discussion, and many points of view were expressed by the participants. No attempt is made in this Monograph to provide an exact reproduction of the discussion. Rather, the material is organized and integrated in a way meaningful to the author and reflects something of his understanding of the topic.

HISTORICAL REVIEW

Psychic trauma held Freud's attention throughout his scientific explorations of neurosis from the time Josef Breuer told him

1

about Anna O. In his earliest writings in *Studies on Hysteria* (1895), he stated that hysterical symptoms could be understood only if they were traced to earlier experiences that had a traumatic effect on the individual. He added, in his own contribution to that book, that the traumata are always related to the patient's sexual life. The response to the original trauma was usually not obvious, but the effects of the trauma would manifest themselves later, when the traumatic experience was revived as a memory, and this characteristically occurred after puberty. The intensity of the stimulus or the absence of abreactive channels of discharge determined whether an experience was traumatic. Freud conceptualized the intrapsychic events taking place with a trauma as a breach in the stimulus barrier, the function of which was to keep excitation at a low optimal level. It is instructive to note that in his earliest works, although he conceived of trauma as the important genetic factor in all neuroses, Freud's view was wide enough for him to add that not all traumata produced neuroses: ". . . a healthy psychical mechanism has other methods of dealing with the affect of a psychical trauma even if motor reaction and reaction by words are denied to it—namely by working it over associatively and by producing contrasting ideas" (1893, p. 37).

Following logically from the concept that absence of sufficient abreactive channels produced the heightened levels of excitation in a traumatic situation, Freud began to develop his first formulations of conflict and repression. In the *Studies on Hysteria,* he wrote that, in order for hysterical symptoms to develop, ". . . an incompatibility should develop between the ego and some idea presented to it. The actual traumatic moment, then, is the one at which the incompatibility forces itself up on the ego and at which the latter decides on the repudiation of the incompatible idea" (1895, pp. 122-123).

This view underwent change later, with the revision of his anxiety theory in 1925. The traumatic moment could then no longer be considered the moment of repression; rather, repression became a reaction to the traumatic experience.

Jones, in his biography of Freud (1953), has described the painful realization and self-exploration forced upon Freud when he had to face the awareness that the sexual seductions in his patients' associations were not all reports of real events. In addition, Jones described the creative leap forward this produced in establishing the important role of sexual wishes and fantasies in neurosogenesis. As a result of this shift, external realistic trauma was replaced in importance by infantile sexual wishes and fantasies. As it came to full appreciation that these wishes and fantasies were universal, the focus of attention shifted from their mere existence in an individual to the individual's reaction to those wishes and fantasies. In other words, it became increasingly important to understand the strengths and weaknesses of the psychic apparatus on which the traumatic excitations impinged.

As theory became more sophisticated, a time factor was added to Freud's definition of trauma. In the *Introductory Lectures* (1916-1917), he defined it as ". . . an experience which within a short period of time presents the mind with an increase of stimulus too powerful to be dealt with or worked off in the normal way . . ." (p. 275).

Soon after, in *Beyond the Pleasure Principle* (1920) he added to this definition certain psychic operations that would eventually be understood as ego functions. Thus, he stressed two factors in psychic trauma: the intensity of the stimulus, and the degree of preparedness of the stimulus barrier. In relation to the latter, he considered that the breach in the barrier caused by trauma was due to a lack of preparedness for the anxiety, and one reason for this lack of preparedness was a failure to hypercathect the systems that were to receive the stimulus first. As a result they would be rendered helpless in binding the incoming excitations, and lead to a state of flooding of the mental apparatus with excessive stimuli.

With the development of the structural theory, Freud (1926) spoke of traumatic situations as experiences of helplessness and nonsatisfaction, which develop in the face of mounting stimulation reaching unpleasurable levels with no outlet for discharge. Automatic (traumatic) anxiety in *experienced* states of danger accompanied by a sense of helplessness was contrasted with signal anxiety, an actively produced response on the part of the ego to the *threat* of danger. The purpose of the latter was to avoid the danger before it occurred and thus avoid the traumatic situation

and automatic anxiety. Freud also outlined the well-known series
of displacements of the danger situation from the danger itself
(originally based on the model of birth), to the loss of the pro-
tecting mother, to the loss of the mother's love, then the loss of
the penis, and finally the loss of love of the superego. The essence
of the danger is the ego's sense of helplessness in the face of
mounting excitation with which it cannot deal, whether the excitation is external or internal in origin. The helplessness of the
ego and the ego's success or failure in dealing with mounting excitation were at this juncture of Freud's theory-building an implicit part of psychic trauma. The ego's strength in many of its
functions, e.g., anticipation, memory, motor control, judgment,
etc., as well as specific ego weaknesses or sensitivities based on past
history, would determine whether a stimulus would or would not
be traumatic. It is therefore not surprising that most psychic traumata occur during the first five years of life, when the ego is in a
process of maturing and is of necessity weak.

For the same reason, contributions to the understanding of
psychic trauma since Freud have come largely from the field of
child analysis and the observation of children. Many contributions emphasize the child's psychic state prior to the trauma as
most important in understanding the outcome of the trauma.
Factors in a child's life which hinder ego development will increase the child's vulnerability to trauma, and Anna Freud (1965)
has demonstrated that those ego functions which have most recently emerged are most vulnerable to regression in the face of
psychic trauma. One special area of interest among the determinants of ego development is the effectiveness of the mother in
her role as a protector, and the play of her anxieties as they affect
the developing child. The possibilities here for aiding the child's
ego development or hindering it are great, depending on the
quality of mothering.

A number of analysts (notably Greenacre, 1950, 1952a, 1952b)
have drawn attention to the importance of the relationship between psychic trauma and the libidinal phase of development in
which it occurs. Certain traumata are likely to have more of an
impact in certain phases than in others. A castration threat may
be traumatic in the phallic phase, but not in an earlier oral phase.

It was Greenacre's suggestion that this specificity of trauma to phase development will determine whether the libidinization of the dominant phase of the moment will be reinforced, or whether a regression to an earlier libidinal phase will occur.

Traumata have been differentiated in a number of ways. Some investigators have written about deprivation trauma as opposed to overstimulation trauma. Spitz (1951) has shown that an optimal level of external stimulation is necessary for healthy psychic development, and some would therefore say that deprivation beyond this optimal minimal level constitutes a trauma. Ernst Kris (1956) differentiated shock trauma from strain trauma and introduced those terms to the psychoanalytic literature. But it is interesting to find that Freud, as early as the *Studies on Hysteria,* spoke of trauma being caused by a single major event or by a number of partial traumata which produce their effect by summation.

This Section of the Kris Study Group decided to work from clinical material, using detailed analytic data concerning traumatic experiences as they emerged in the course of a therapeutic analysis, or in the close observation of children, as the springboard for discussion. Traumatic experiences were to be delineated, and our intention was to follow the observable effects, both immediate and long term, thereby attempting to understand the determining factors and their interplay in producing the symptomatic end-results. The nature of the traumata we examined varied a good deal and included the following:

> Prolonged, overwhelming, and severe threat to life and dignity, as seen in concentration camp victims.

> Forced sexual seduction in childhood.

> Parental rejection due to the death of a parent and due to poor mothering.

> Physical illness or defect in a child.

> Observing the anatomical difference between sexes at a vulnerable age.

A few preliminary observations might help orient the reader for the data to follow. Although each contribution included a specific trauma which was expected to become the focus of the discussion, it soon became apparent that what was presented as a single trauma proved to be but one part of a complex interwoven fabric of traumata. Delineating a single trauma was quite impossible. A child's loss of a parent at an early age may well be traumatic, but, as well as suffering this immense loss, he may lose the surviving parent emotionally because of his or her mourning or depression. He is also deprived of the vital functions the lost parent would ordinarily have provided for maturation and development in ongoing years. All of these are interconnected possible traumata, but different from one another. Which is most important in an individual case can only be determined in analysis. A number of such observations led to the conclusion that traumata do not occur singly, but in clusters.

The distinction between shock trauma and strain trauma was discussed, as well as their interrelationship. We questioned whether shock trauma and stress had different effects on an individual. The concept of these two types of trauma is not universally accepted, although this study group did find it a useful and helpful distinction. Ernst Kris accepted the distinction, as noted above, but Anna Freud (1964) and Robert Waelder (1965) prefer to limit the term trauma to the acute shock variety in order to maintain its meaning more clearly. The differences between trauma due to deprivation and that due to excessive stimulation also commanded some attention. The importance of the pretraumatic personality was evident in most of the discussion, with the one notable exception of concentration camp victims, where it seemed to play no role. The libidinal phase and stage of ego development at the time of the trauma also emerged as significant. Differences in impact when a trauma was due to wishful fantasy as opposed to a realistic experience were noted. The reaction of the individual at the time of the traumatic event was not decisive in determining whether the event would be traumatic. It is thus characteristic that a child's reaction to the death of a parent may not appear to be overwhelming. Usually, events are judged as traumatic in retrospect. In this connection, another important finding was the existence of a latency period of varying duration between the traumatic event and the presence of discernible effects. This characterized all the cases studied.

An observation of a more general nature is worth noting. The discussions indicated how very easily the term "psychic trauma" may be confused with the concept of conflict or with pathogenicity. There are examples of this in some of the cases to follow. One last point must be emphasized, although it seems deceptively simple. Events that are traumatic are traumatic to the individual who experiences them, and they are not traumatic merely because, in the eye of the empathic analytic observer, they seem to be so. As Anna Freud (1965) made amply clear, a painful event in and of itself is not traumatic. Only when its meaning for the individual is understood in relation to the level of ego development and to his individual developmental background can it be evaluated as traumatic or not.

From these observations it is evident that this Kris Study Group struggled with many of the same ideas as had Freud and his followers years ago. If the Group did no more than raise or refine more pertinent questions to be answered in the future, its work has been very worthwhile.

MASSIVE TRAUMA OVERWHELMING THE
EGO'S RESOURCES

Presentation 1: The Survivor Syndrome

Dr. William G. Niederland, together with Dr. Martin Wangh, discussed some of the findings derived from their work with survivors of Nazi concentration camps. Niederland had seen hundreds of such patients over a 15-year period, although never in analysis, and had found a symptom picture displayed with such great regularity that the term "survivor syndrome" was coined to refer to it. It is important to note that this syndrome was present regardless of the premorbid personality of the patient, and did no seem to be significantly influenced by his previous background and individual history. Without exception, all people exposed to the concentration camp experiences (i.e., the "death camps" as distinguished from the "labor camps") showed marked after-effects of the traumatic experiences, the intensity of which was so great that none escaped without serious personality damage. The nature of the concentration camp trauma consisted of chronic starvation (often no more than 400 calories daily intake), physical debilitation and emaciation, and the ever-present threat to life. There was also no acknowledgment of the individual's existence. All cause-and-effect relationships ceased; events took place without reason. Prisoners existed without any rights at all, standing in total mental nakedness, desperate, and unable to rely on anything or anyone. These conditions produced a new "security," namely, the security of certain destruction. The jokes which sprang up about this seemed heartlessly cruel to newcomers. Constant pervasive threats of torture and death had to be met with absolute control and suppression of both aggressive retaliatory reactions and altruistic impulses. Isolation from and destruction of the family was commonplace, but appropriate affective and motor reaction was not permissible. This immersion in an atmosphere of relentless coercion, destruction, and death produced the experience of leading a "living dead" existence without hope.

There was a characteristic symptom-free interval following liberation at the end of the war—that is, after the cessation of the traumatic events—before the symptoms of the later "survivor syndrome" appeared. The symptoms appeared months or years after arrival in the United States. As long as the survivors believed that some of their missing families might reappear, and as long as they were exposed to the many hardships of adjustment to a new way of life, they were relatively symptom-free. When hope for family survival was given up and adjustment to the new way of life was more or less accomplished, the postpersecution symptomatology emerged. Niederland concluded from this that the traumatic experiences and perceptions were repressed for the duration of the emergency and thereafter dealt with by denial, repression, or isolation, and that affects either were somatized or emerged directly as anxiety or depression.

When symptoms did emerge in the United States, the predominant complaint was found to be anxiety associated with fears of renewed persecution, sleep disturbances, "re-run" nightmares, and transparent phobias (this last, a phobic response to a current stimulus that evokes memories of concentration camp experiences). There were disturbances of cognition and memory, and disorientation between the present and the period of persecution, especially upon awakening. Chronic depressive states covering the spectrum from masochistic character changes to psychotic depression were most characteristic. So consistent was the finding of severe guilt reactions in the survivors that it eventually could be called "survivor guilt." Mourning had not been possible in the camps, and the resolution of guilt feelings was therefore not accomplished. Instead, what occurred at the time was an incorporation of the lost object and an identification with the dead that produced a regressive state akin to marasmus and psychic stupor. The prisoners spoke of one another in this state as "walking or shuffling corpses." Compounding the problem of survivor guilt was a widespread identification with the destructive atmosphere of the camp and a heightened psychological interest in death, all of which contributed to the disturbances in the sense of identity. In the survivor syndrome, guilt and shame produced social withdrawal and grieving. Object relations were thin and schizoid. Regressive methods of dealing with aggression were employed, producing a psychotic-like, paranoid, or hypochondriacal picture. Psychosomatic disorders also formed part of the syndrome.

Survivor guilt, the most outstanding morbid factor in the survivor syndrome, is considered a form of pathological mourning. Behind the self-reproaches were found repressed rage against lost parents for failing to protect them from persecution. Significant ego and superego changes were usually in evidence among those who denied aftereffects. Common among these were a disturbed reality sense, a shaky sense of self, loss of object constancy, and depersonalization phenomena.

Discussion

These cases of concentration camp survivors are unique examples of traumatic impact on the psychic apparatus, in that the nature of the pretraumatic personality had no influence on the symptomatic outcome. The overwhelming intensity of the stimulus and its long duration would seem to have shattered all previously existing ego resources. None were able to escape the

traumatic impact. One should note the latency period between
the liberation and the outbreak of symptoms, for it will become
a characteristic feature as this study unfolds. The fact that mourning was not possible in the concentration camp made it impossible to separate from the inner love objects, thereby facilitating
identification with the dead. The camp experiences also reawak-
ened particularly primitive sadomasochistic impulses in the prisoners which further limited their ego's capacity to neutralize
drives, as can be seen in the symptoms which appeared.

CHILDHOOD TRAUMA IMPOSED FROM THE OUTSIDE

Presentation 2: A Case of a Childhood Sexual Trauma

This case demonstrates the effects of a specific childhood sexual
trauma on adult behavior in general, and on the transference
situation in particular. Defenses against submission, passivity, and
femininity emerged in dramatic form and proved to be genetically
related to the trauma, which was reconstructed in the analysis.

The patient, a woman in her early thirties, came to analysis
because she either chose impotent men as her romantic partners
or destroyed promising relationships with suitable men. Her quiet
ineffectual father had been dominated by her mother, a psychotic
woman who became a physical invalid in her later years. When
the patient was a child, the mother beat her frequently with very
little provocation. Battles between the parents and between the
mother and neighbors were commonplace. The mother had not
wanted to marry, and had fled back to her own parents' home
shortly after marrying. Only after much coaxing on the part
of her husband and her parents, was she persuaded to resume
her married life. There had been an older brother who died
before the patient's birth.

A major traumatic experience occurred when she was four
years old, at the outbreak of the second World War. At that time,
because of the bombings, she was evacuated, along with many
other children, to the countryside, and thus separated from her
parents for two years. Until her evacuation, the patient shared the
parental bedroom, and was lifted out of her crib and tenderly
placed in bed beside her mother each morning by her father as he

left for work. Following the two-year evacuation period, her mother brought her back home because she had been neglected and mistreated, and possibly because of her own loneliness, for the father was in hiding. She spent the last years of the war, which were replete with memories or fears of bombings and shelters, at home. Until the age of 10 she did very well in school. Then she lost interest in scholastic work, rebelled against her mother and teachers alike, refused to go to school, and became intensely interested in athletics—especially in a body-contact sport usually associated with men. Long hours over a stretch of years devoted to practice made her an outstanding player.

Punishments of all sorts, especially floggings and whippings, held an increasing fascination and excitement for her. Her first boy friend was a fellow athlete, to whom she behaved most submissively and compliantly. In contrast, she could coldly walk out on her mother or father, even at times when they were in great physical distress. Coldness became a source of pride for her. When she was 19, her father died, and she left her mother to join her boy friend in Israel, where he had emigrated. She professed no sense of loss at her father's death, nor did she feel guilty at leaving her invalid mother alone. To her surprise, her boy friend was not at all the way she had imagined him. She found him narcissistic, competitive with her, and even openly cruel. She finally left him, found a job which made her self-supporting, and soon began to create fictitious stories about her background, using assumed names. She ceased this imposture shortly after she formed a more lasting relationship with an American. For some time she resisted his pressures to become involved. When he made clear that his intentions were serious, she impulsively broke off the relationship and fled to the United States, where she had long wanted to settle. Alone in a strange country, she joined an American athletic group where she befriended a man whom she knew had severe sexual problems. She nevertheless married him against professional advice she had sought at the time. The marriage was short and stormy and ended in divorce. He was a masochistic sexual pervert with severely delayed or absent ejaculation.

Very early in her analysis she made it clear that she intended to take control. She refused to associate or to respond to questions. Characteristic was her statement, "This is my analysis, and I'll talk about what I choose to talk about." The intensity of her hostility and how long she could sustain it were most impressive. She accepted interpretations unmoved and in silence. Never would she allow it to appear that she wanted anything of the analyst. If she needed a change of hour, for example, rather than ask for it, she would angrily announce, "I won't be here Monday!" When with boy friends, she would on occasion playfully grab for their genitals or, if on intimate terms, would bite the penis during fellatio, sometimes causing bleeding. Submission to a man was intolerable for her, and she often tried to disrupt and annoy in the analytic treatment setting. The second year of analysis was marked by one crisis after another. She threatened suicide when a boy friend broke off with her; she frequently threatened to break off treatment; she fantasied lodging complaints through a professional group to censure the analyst. Finally, she accidentally became pregnant and was about to permit a primitive home abortion. This last crisis required the analyst's active intervention, which led her to ask the man to marry her. When he agreed, she chose to keep the pregnancy.

She described "stamping out" positive fantasies and dreams about the analyst. It was after giving birth to her son and while attending a meeting on hypnosis that she became frightened by the idea of being in someone's power. The analyst interpreted this as part of her fear of relinquishing control of her thoughts in analysis. A struggle followed about whether to report a transference fantasy or quit treatment. When the first fantasies about the analyst began to emerge, she was able to work with them to some extent by focusing on her own associations rather than on the analyst, whom she constantly watched for reactions. The teasing and provocative behavior eased, and a therapeutic alliance was formed.

In brief, it became possible to reconstruct the main facts of two wartime evacuations, not just one. The first was connected with a screen memory of a garden in blazing color in December. Her stay there, however, was interrupted suddenly, and she recalled that she was told never to speak of it or to visit the place again. She was then placed with a second family in the same small town. Her first recollection of this placement was a memory of standing the little boy in the family under a sunflower in their garden, and rubbing sunflower seeds into his hair so that he could not get them out. It was this second placement that was connected with memories of neglect (for example, she developed nits in her hair) and with a memory of being forced by the older girls in the household to get on her knees and pray almost daily. Several years after returning to her parents' home, while spending a pleasant summer in the country with relatives, she became preoccupied with the story of the Garden of Eden and, while relating this during her session, she recalled thinking of the first placement as the Garden of Eden. Several times she reported dreams, shadowy memories, and fantasies regarding excited old men pictured as gripping the arms of their chairs while she was sitting between their legs on the floor. Finally she recalled that she had returned home briefly between the two wartime placements, and while at home she set fire to her own hair. It was possible now to reconstruct a sexual trauma to which she had been subjected in her first placement, probably by the elderly man of the house. The experience most probably involved fellatio accompanied by the detail of having semen in her hair. She reacted to this trauma by developing intense defenses against femininity and against passivity. The conflicts were repressed during latency, but erupted again at age 10, as much of what emerged later in analysis indicated, leading both to her rebellion against identification with her mother and to the development of the fantasy that she had a phallus. A great deal of analytic work was given over to her castration fears, her penis envy, her terror of helplessness and passivity, and her sadomasochistic preoccupations—all of which led to her own awareness of improved object relationships. She nevertheless resented that this improvement meant that she was submitting to the analyst. She eventually left treatment prematurely, fearful of giving up her image of a degraded analyst and of acknowledging her positive feelings for him.

Discussion

The clinical data bring out the fact that this patient had experienced several traumata in childhood: the sudden separation from her parents at the age of four; two years spent away from home at that early age; the sadomasochistic struggles between mother and daughter and between the parents; the overexposure, overstimulation and primal-scene experiences implicit in the sleeping arrangements; and the specific sexual trauma reconstructed in the analysis. It would be doing an injustice to the clinical material to say that only a single trauma had occurred. Rather, traumata of different types which were interrelated had occurred together. One could say she had had a clustering of traumata in her childhood, some of the shock variety and some of the stress variety. The daily sadomasochistic climate in the home, and the two years away from home, would constitute the stress trauma; the sexual experience at age four, a shock trauma. It would follow, then, that stress traumata in this case affected her character structure, as seen in her reenactment of the sadomasochistic tensions in the transference and constant threats to quit treatment. The shock trauma was more clearly related to her symptoms in the sexual sphere. Difficulties in submitting to rules, in forming object relationships, and her basic distrust of love objects were related to both types of trauma. Rigidity on the couch, especially in response to interpretations, has, in the opinion of several members of the study group, regularly been related to primal scene experiences.

A specific characterological aspect in this case related to the beatings during her childhood. It was the experience of one member of the study group that beatings tend to fixate libidinal cathexis on the body surface and to produce the sexualization of body activity (prominently present in this case). People subjected to beatings tend to heighten the experience of body tension, building it to a peak without discharge, in order to feel intact. Without this tension in relation to the object, there is a feeling of dissolution. These elements were present in the case material, not all of which has been included here. The patient's self representation was poor and inconsistent (e.g., her need to create a fictitious background for herself). This was demonstrated by her use of libidinization of motion and states of heightened tension and intense rage in the service of holding on to a shaky sense of self. When the defenses broke down, depersonalization and clouded states developed. Her tolerance for intrapsychic conflict was very low; she tended to feel little guilt, but rather projected hostility and criticism onto love objects. Put another way, the low tolerance for intrapsychic conflict was matched by a very high tolerance for interpersonal conflict.

It was concluded that traumata occur in clusters and not singly; that shock- and stress traumata are interrelated and possibly never occur apart from one another; that stress-and-strain trauma seems to affect character structure more, whereas shock trauma seems to affect symptom formation more—although there is a good deal of overlap. Object relations are affected by both shock- and stress traumata. It should be noted that there was a latency period between the time of greatest trauma (age four) and the outbreak of is discernible effects (age 10).

Presentation 3: Shock Trauma Occurring during
a Child's Analysis

This case report was first presented by Drs. Marianne Kris and Albert J. Solnit to The New York Psychoanalytic Society on January 11, 1966. Because it offered an opportunity to explore the effects of an acute shock trauma taking place while the child patient was in analysis, Drs. Kris and Solnit were invited to present their material to the study group and join in the discussion. The case was unusual in that the previous history, current situation, developmental and maturational pressures, and analytic situation were known when the trauma occurred.

Margaret's analysis provided the authors with an opportunity to examine an acute trauma against the background of a stressful early development created by a significant incompatibility between the child and her mother. The mother-child pair were subjects in a longitudinal study at the Child Study Center of Yale University, a unique advantage, in that extensive information from birth was available. The child had been in analysis for some three months when the traumatic incident occurred. Margaret's mother had a lifelong yearning for gifts from parental figures and felt that men had all the advantages over women. Sexual relations disgusted her, and the first seven months of her pregnancy were accompanied by severe nausea and vomiting. She was afraid her vomiting would hurt the baby and even feared the child would be a vomiter after birth. Because she always lost interest in anything she wanted once she finally got it, she was afraid she might lose interest in her baby. Labor was long and exhausting, and after 20 hours, spinal anesthesia and forceps were used to overcome the uterine inertia. The mother was elated by the experience, guilt-ridden because of the sense of satisfaction it gave her, and also felt the birth had damaged her.

From the second day of life, Margaret had two qualities of response that manifested themselves in various ways throughout her infancy. The first was poor tolerance for tactile, kinesthetic, and auditory stimuli, all of which evoked a jarring, startle reaction. In addition, her motor responses to local stimuli tended to be global or generalized. These traits made it difficult to hold and cuddle Margaret, especially for her mother, who was afraid she would damage the baby. The mother's care interacted with Margaret's neonatal characteristics in a way that interfered with the development of a mutual intimate physical closeness. These sensitivities diminished somewhat as Margaret developed, particularly her intolerance for tactile and kinesthetic stimuli. By the time she was three months old, she comforted herself more effectively by handling a diaper or looking a toy than her mother did by holding her. This and other observations suggested that the intolerances noted above were later complicated by an intolerance of direct passive experience in relation to the need-satisfying object. When the child could become active, the painful discomforts were minimized.

To hold the infant closely was uncomfortable for the mother, because it represented a tempting but threatening outlet for her erotized aggression. She even managed to relegate some of her parental role to the pediatrician, with herself as a go-between who merely followed instructions. When the child was held and touched and manipulated by the mother in the feeding situation, Margaret's discomfort was increased. This led to the utilization of the child's increasing activity and motor development in the service of defensive adaptation against the danger of painful passive experiences. Her capacity to recognize and organize her impressions of the environment, in advance of her age, reflected her good endowment. This capacity was also used in the service of defense and adaptation, and she became sharply aware and controlling of the threatening environment. In the use of visual recognition and memory of new place, this was especially clear.

In the second and third years, the child's persistent use of imitative behavior when in new and frightening situations seemed to reveal the difficulties of the earlier experiences with the mother. Imitation was used mainly to satisfy the mother with good performance, and at the same time kept the mother at a safe distance. The persistent imitative behavior suggested an arrest in the development of identification as an adaptive function of the ego. The authors viewed this arrest as a vulnerability which could express itself in the context of a threatening trauma.

In Margaret's second year of life the awkwardness and stiffness of her body in play indicated an inhibition in motor skills. The need to comply with her mother's demands and so to avoid danger, as well as the fear of losing control of an apparatus that tended earlier to overflow in its responses, produced stiffness and a lack of grace, although motor skills were age adequate. Margaret's facial expression, strikingly mobile in the neonate period, had become sober and relatively immobile. Because flexibility is considered to be one of the factors that can increase the capacity for coping with trauma-threatening situations, these developments in Margaret's pattern of response were clearly limiting.

The traumatic incident occurred when Margaret was three and a half years old. She had become provocatively and regressively boisterous in the back seat of the car, making wild animal noises, which her mother called "African sounds." In the past, the mother had used the word "African" successfully to stop such unruly behavior, but on this day it did not work. Enraged, her mother stopped the car in the middle of a swampy, uninhabited area and commanded the child to get out of the car. According to the mother, the child promised to behave, was again ordered out, dissolved into tears, and was then strapped to the front seat of the car. Margaret's version differed. She told the analyst that she got out of the car and cried before her mother permitted her back in.

The incident took place when Margaret was coping with specific developmental tasks—namely, adapting to an eight-month-old sibling; dealing with progressive phallic and oedipal tasks of development as well as certain anal regressive impulses; mastering the separation from her mother brought about by nursery school attendance. She had been in psychoanalytic treatment for three months when this trauma occurred, and she had recently learned that the analyst's wife was soon to have a child, which would cause him to miss several appointments. During the same period of time, Margaret's mother was concerned about having an automobile accident, distrusting both her skill as a driver and her control over her impulses.

Margaret, immediately after the marshland trauma, allowed herself to be strapped into the front seat of the car and became a good, "frozen" child. Her overwhelming fear of abandonment and castration were from that time repeatedly played out in thinly disguised ways in the analytic treatment. The analysis indicated that the fear of being left in a deserted area, helpless in the face of her own feelings of wildness, had reached the point of inundating the child. For several months she could approach the memory of this event only after playing out scenes in which girls were damaged following separation from their parents.

Discussion

The report focused on one single trauma, the marshland episode. But in the discussion, many other traumata were quickly brought up as significant to the development of the pathology. In fact, the entire year prior to the marshland episode might be considered the patient's "traumatic year." Whether the mother's "abandoning her" at the time of the birth of the sibling might be the more significant trauma—revived in the transference when the analyst's baby was born—is also a possibility. If so, the marshland experience might have represented the patient's need to provoke and relive the earlier trauma—an abandonment by the mother. This formulation resembles the process in older girls described by Greenacre (1950) in her paper on "The Prepuberty Trauma in Girls."

In the discussion Dr. Solnit emphasized the difficulty encountered in comparing the impact of a visible external threat with an internal danger (for example, intense fear of object loss may appear without external evidence of threat). He felt, nevertheless, that what was most overt and visible was usually clearest and least ambiguous. Dr. Kris agreed that many of the other factors were clearly hardship or strain traumata; yet the marshland incident was the most striking and most significant event seen clinically. She felt that Margaret did provoke her mother in the marshland incident, but probably to evoke only a spanking and not the abandonment that resulted. Without the abandonment threat, Margaret would not have been traumatized. Dr. Solnit added that the mother's aggression was under poor control while she was driving the car, and her rage was beyond anything Margaret had expected or experienced prior to that time.

A child's reaction to a trauma depends in large part on the libidinal phase and on the level of ego development attained at the time of the trauma. An older child might well have handled the marshland episode without a traumatic reaction. But when it was suggested that having a male analyst intensified Margaret's oedipal strivings, with the result that there was a regressive movement to a preoedipal fixation to the mother, Dr. Kris strongly disagreed, proposing instead that the analyst's being a man had allowed the expression of this child's forbidden wishes and had acted to diminish regressive trends. This is in keeping with Greenacre's suggestion that phase-appropriate trauma helps libidinize the dominant phase of the moment and diminishes the chances for regression.

The evidence favoring the view that the marshland incident was specifically traumatic included the following: It was a violent incident which disrupted the child's behavior in an overwhelming manner. She repeatedly tried to master her reaction to it by bringing up disguised partial versions of it. When the event was gradually reconstructed by verbalization and dramatic play, she grew pale and preoccupied and had trouble leaving those sessions. A screen memory developed, demonstrated by her speaking in a pressured way about her sibling's birth, to screen and limit the traumatic impact of her mother's abandonment in the marshland. The screen offered relief in the knowledge that this earlier abandonment led to the mother's safe return.

Regarding the different effects of shock trauma and strain trauma, Dr. Solnit suggested that the former can be recognized by the psychic disorganization that takes place, often following very rapidly upon the experience. It has long-lasting effects, particularly in the area of defense. He believed that children who have experienced considerable strain trauma are most likely to react with shock trauma. Repeated low grade strain traumas promote the development of an inflexibility in defensive reactions. Not only does strain trauma promote the development of rigid ego defenses, but it renders the individual more vulnerable to shock trauma. Such a person does not have at his disposal the repertoire of ego defenses necessary for a flexible adaptation to challenges of a varied nature that may come from the environment or from inner drives. Dr. Kris stressed that acute disorganization, which is an essential aspect of shock trauma, does not occur with stress trauma. Margaret's outstanding characteristic was the rigidity of her defenses, which rendered her unable to handle stresses in a versatile way, as a normal child might. This inflexibility was the result of an ongoing stress-and-strain trauma, which produced her special adaptation to her mother. Threatening and angry experiences often occurred with her mother, but the marshland experience reached an intensity that was overwhelming, disrupting ego capacities in a continuing way, as could be seen in her helpless appearance at the time, as well as her blanched appearance of panic when the episode was relived in analysis. Margaret's subsequent distrust of her own behavior unless her mother indicated approval strongly suggests a disruption of former ego capacities.

Margaret did not develop an infantile neurosis. Instead, there was a narrowing of her ego's repertoire of activity. She submitted to her mother and suppressed and repressed her affects and fantasies. The earlier deficiencies in tactile and kinesthetic reactions contributed to a lack of tenderness in her object relationships, to an intolerance for passive gratification, and to attempts at overcontrol of her body and her environment. This deficiency of tactile and kinesthetic experiences, coupled with too many painful experiences with her mother in her first few years of life, produced an obstacle in the child's turning from proprioceptive awareness to a balanced sensory awareness of the outer world. She adapted to her mother's apprehensiveness and her own perceptual hypersensitivity, but this adaptation served to constrict her development. Id and ego development were restrained by excessive use of control, as were the id-ego interactions so necessary for the differentiation of the ego functions.

Whether Margaret's intolerance of kinesthetic sensations, already noted on her second day of life, was due to constitutional equipment or to a specific neonatal response to the environment could not be completely answered. Dr. Solnit felt that this child's sensitivities probably fell within the normal range, and it was only by virtue of the inappropriate maternal handling that they moved into the sphere of the pathological. He recalled that Margaret's mother could not tolerate a wriggling child, and, as a result, she and the child made an "implicit deal" to establish a mutually acceptable distance. For example, the child fed herself with the bottle. Later similar "deals" were made, focusing on areas often prone to interpersonal conflict, such as toilet training.

Imitation and identification constituted another area of great interest in this case. Imitation is a normal forerunner of more mature identification and involves magical and total identity rather than realistic and selective similarity. It implies a relative lack of ego involvement because no real internalization has taken place, and the self representation does not take on lasting qualities belonging to the object. Imitation falls away as quickly as it develops, whereas identification is more or less lasting. Generally, imitative behavior begins at the end of the first or the beginning of the second year of life, but Margaret's imitative behavior was prominent at 10 months and did not diminish, suggesting an arrest in the development of the process of identification. Her imitations were caricatures tending to ridicule her mother. The child's separation anxiety also contributed to the difficulty in identifying with the mother. Follow-up studies showed that she had partially mastered this problem with identification, especially as it related to separation from her mother.

Dr. Solnit offered a speculative thesis regarding the difference in the effects produced by a trauma resulting from deprivation as opposed to a trauma resulting from excessive stimulation: De-

privation trauma was apt to lead to arrested instinctual development. Trauma resulting from excessive stimulation seems more
likely to cause arrested ego development. Also, deprivation trauma
results in an inadequacy (not arrest) of ego development, leaving
the individual subject to become overwhelmed by the drives.

The authors, independent of the study group observation, suggested that longitudinal observations reduced the tendency to
view traumatic events as single, acute, shock-like experiences, for
the more one knows about the person's inner and outer life, the
more one can discern significant related events and conflicts sur-
rounding the specific trauma. Again the clustering of traumata,
as opposed to single occurrences, would appear to be characteristic.

Drs. Kris and Solnit offered the following criteria as guidelines
for the concept of shock trauma: The phenomenon reflects a
reaction to an inner or outer demand or stimulus that is to a
significant degree experienced as overwhelming to the mediating
functions of the ego. The "overwhelming" quality includes some
or all of the following: It is sudden, disruptive, and pierces or
rends the stimulus barrier. It paralyzes or immobilizes the subject, rendering him helpless. It results in disorganization of feelings, thoughts, and behavior, and the disturbances in affective
reactions ranging from numbness to emotional storm. It produces
regressive phenomena and severe inhibition. The ego, suddenly
deprived of certain autonomous functions, is depleted of conflict-
free energy. Shock trauma produces physical symptoms reflecting
autonomous dysfunction (blanching, diarrhea, vomiting, etc.).
Finally, there is a characteristic recovery pattern for shock trauma.

In summary, once more we found a clustering of traumata
rather than a single isolated trauma whose effects could be traced.
There was strong evidence supporting the view that stress (strain)
trauma is responsible for increasing the individual's vulnerability
to shock trauma, that this comes about because of the consequent
rigidity of the ego defenses. Margaret demonstrated this rigidity
and narrowing of repertoire of the ego's range of responses in her
fixation on imitation and lack of progressive movement toward
mature identification. An intriguing suggestion emerged—with
somewhat less support from clinical material—that overstimulation trauma produces an arrest of ego development and depriva-

tion trauma gives rise to arrested drive development, as well as inadequacy (as opposed to arrest) of ego development.

Presentation 4: Death of a Parent Occurring during a Child's Analysis

The following case report, like the previous one, concerns a child who experienced a severe shock trauma while in analysis. It involved the unexpected, sudden death of his father, shortly after the child's analysis began. Because of these unique circumstances, it offered an unusual opportunity to examine the pretraumatic personality structure as an aid in understanding the child's attempts to cope with the trauma of losing an important object, and from this to trace how the posttraumatic behavior patterns were influenced by the trauma.

This boy entered analysis at age four and a half for two main reasons: because he wildly attacked other children and because he frequently dressed up like a girl, an activity which began with an interest in his mother's high heels at the age of two and a half. He wore her necklace, underwear, and nightgown, used her make-up, took on feminine body movements, and pretended to be a queen or a princess. His father disapproved so strongly that knowledge of this behavior had to be kept from him. Then, six weeks after the boy started analysis, his father suddenly died in a train crash.

The patient's only sibling was born when he was three and a quarter years old. During the pregnancy he became very destructive of his toys and other objects. After the birth he was cruel to his newborn brother and soon developed a sleep disturbance: he had difficulty in falling asleep and awoke early. Because he was afraid of the dark, he wanted to cuddle with his father, and insisted on a night light. His mother's breasts fascinated him, and he tried whenever possible to see her in some state of undress. One favorite activity was wrestling with his father, an activity the father greatly enjoyed; in the midst of the wrestling, the father would often kiss him affectionately. It should be mentioned that both the father's and grandfather's businesses were related to feminine fashions. The father was proud of his independence from his own father and of his considerable business success.

In an effort to improve his relationship with the patient he
undertook psychotherapy when his son entered analysis. He felt
too impatient with his son and sensed that his anger on discover-
ing transvestite behavior made the problem worse. The weekend
before he died, he reported to his wife that he was able to thor-
oughly enjoy the company of his two boys, despite their noisy,
provocative behavior. His new freedom from rancor had impressed his wife. Following one of his first therapeutic sessions,
however, he demonstrated a frightening degree of carelessness.
While lighting a bonfire in his backyard, in full view of his wife
and the patient, he poured kerosene into the flames, risking a
small explosion. His wife was furious, pounded on a window to
attract his attention and, in so doing, broke it. Fragments of glass
in her hand required a trip to the hospital. The patient witnessed
the entire scene.

The mother, who had a tendency to transvestism and exhibi-
tionism, was given to impulsive pinching of the patient's buttocks,
saying, "This is mine, this is mine!" She carried these assaults to
the point of producing black and blue bruises. At these times she
would also grind her teeth, which on three occasions resulted in
chipping a tooth. She would say, "I could eat you up! I eat
boys." Later on the patient identified with this activity, pinching
his own buttocks after bathing and saying, "Mine, mine." Many
of the mother's interests and activities demonstrated her strong
drive to control people and situations and to display a fantasy that
she was complete, male and female, and could do without a man.
As one might imagine, pregnancy and delivery were not to be allowed to interfere with her undergraduate education and examina-
tions, and she saw to it that any interference was minimal. The parental relationship was not a good one; quarrels and fist fights were
frequent and often severe. His mother's tendency to hit his father
stopped only when the father began to strike her back.

Among his assets, this boy had an excellent vocabulary with a
high level of general information. He was overtly affectionate
with relatives and friends, charming and generally serious and
reflective when in company other than his mother's. His span of
attention was considered long, and he had excellent skill in
painting, modeling, and construction. A swimming teacher re-

ported that he was a pleasure to work with because of his persistence and excellent coordination.

The patient showed no reluctance to leaving his mother for the very first analytic session. It was the mother who found it difficult to separate. She tried to whisper to the analyst about the patient's ambivalence—he both wished to tell the doctor and did not want to tell him about touching his penis because it itched. In the session, he concentrated on fingerpaints, making cheerful multicolored blots, and indicated that his favorite color was pink. He was overly preoccupied with neatness as it concerned the play table and his own clothing, but not at all about the floor, even going out of his way to drop globs of paint on it. He never mentioned his concern about his penis, but instead said that his trouble was that other children hate him. He thought the analyst might hate him as his mother hated him. Some of the children hated him because he hit them.

Prior to his father's death, the patient spoke freely in his treatment about his feminine wishes. One day he awoke with a "mermaid feeling." He wanted to be a mermaid, and he wanted to catch a mermaid for his father, whom he felt sure would like one. This led to his expressing his fears of cracks in the floor and to a preoccupation with "tippy block buildings" which, when interpreted as his own sense of feeling tippy—that is, not as strong as he would like to be—produced a rash of aggressive behavior and injury to other children. He used cracks in doorways as a weapon in this activity. Interpretive work helped him to see that in his provocative behavior he was in fact doing the opposite of what he wanted, which was to facilitate making friends.

On hearing the news of his father's death, he did not cry, but said, "I want my Daddy back." He repeated this several times in the next few days. Two and a half hours after learning the news, he admitted to a child in his classroom that he was sad. He also told the analyst a story of the "dark, mysterious night," and about "the black, mysterious things that happened last night," all of which were interpreted as references to his father's death. When another child threatened to kick the analyst, he became protective of the doctor and displayed an unprecedented fatherly friendliness to other children, saying, "I love you, my son," and the like. Other imitations of his father's play, such as wrestling or horseback riding, occurred as well. By the second session, a dramatic regression had occurred. It was displayed in his inability to share crackers with other children and in his inability to sustain the activity of painting. Instead, he mixed paints to create a magic formula to kill people. In the transference there was an increase in his positive attachment, and several times he called the analyst "Daddy."

He projected his sadness onto the doctor, saying, "You are sad that you can't see me every day." Denial of the father's death occurred in the form of small amnesias such as, "Will you have to tell my mother and father?" Magical thinking was more prominent, and the oedipal theme emerged more strikingly. He was going to be king of the world and bomb everything. Yet, no increase in his sexual advances to his mother was noted, and his transvestite behavior at home lessened. Instead, transvestite material appeared for the first time in his analysis. He continued to show an ominous degree of aggression turned on himself. The day prior to his father's death, feeling guilty about something he had done, he had run his head into the wall. A few days after the father's death, he tried to smash his head open and continued to provoke attacks on himself which he then smilingly received. At home he became more aggressive toward his younger brother and could not be prevented from hurting him. Interpreting his jealousy of other children in his nursery class as a form of jealousy to his brother led to his open expression of a wish to be held on his teacher's lap and mothered. Identification with his father continued as he brought his father's umbrella and sunglasses to school, and expressed a wish to bring one of his ties. Sublimations, including painting and block play, suffered a great deal, nearly disappearing for a week in this usually highly productive boy. Six weeks after his father's death, there was still an inhibition which took the form of dissatisfaction with his first and second product, which he wanted to destroy. By the second postbereavement week, one area of sublimation improved beyond the earlier level, that of block building. His castles, parallel to his kingly fantasies, became more complex and sturdier.

In summary, clearest in the trends observed following the death of his father were increases in identification with the father, aggression directed against the self, magical grandiose thinking, the positive relation to the analyst and use of denial of reality. There was, at the same time, deterioration of sublimation, an appearance of undisguised oedipal strivings, and fantasy and play themes centering around the reality of the trauma.

Discussion

Several possible traumata could be delineated in this case: the father's death; the mother's response to the loss; the seductive earlier relationship with the mother; and the impact on the child of the father's personality. In response to the father's death, the mother was gay and energetic and resorted to magical thinking and to primitive identification with the dead husband. Among the important influences prior to the father's death were the mother's seductive behavior to the patient—regarding him as her phallus—and the possibly homosexual coloring to the father's relationship with the boy. These could be viewed as stress traumata on which were superimposed the shock trauma of the father's death. The father's death might possibly be regarded, not as a separate trauma, but as a measure of the way the previous stress (strain) traumata had shaped the child's reaction to that death. But regarding the death as a new trauma superimposed on the old had more solid clinical support because of the evidence of the patient's repeated attempts to work over the wound of the father's death. The relative paucity of spontaneously verbalized sadness and the prominence of denial and displacement are characteristic of children who have lost a parent. The realization of an oedipal-wish fantasy was considered important in coloring the traumatic effect in this case, but the clinical evidence for this was not convincing. How much of the reaction was oedipal in flavor and how much reflected regressive grandiosity is open to question. The specific meaning of death to this boy was also not clear, and the traumatic effects may not be fully known for years.

This case report illustrates the clustering of traumata, and the relative impossibility of tracing a single trauma without reference to other related traumatic experiences. This seemingly single trauma, the death of a parent, also means the absence of that parent for important future development, and often is tantamount to the loss of the surviving parent in the period of mourning that follows. Each of these has a traumatic potential, and which is most significant in a given case requires careful clinical study. The importance of the pretraumatic history emerges very clearly in this case. In fact, without it we would have difficulty understanding the traumatic experience. In this particular case, as in many others, the prehistory involved long-standing stress-and-strain traumata upon which the acute trauma is superimposed, reinforcing the idea that prolonged strain trauma increases the individual's susceptibility to shock trauma.

The following presentations (Presentations 5 and 6) attempt to focus on how the dominant maturational task at the time of the trauma may determine which ego functions will bear the brunt of traumatic impact and thus color the clinical picture which develops.

Presentation 5: Trauma Experienced in the Separation-
Individuation Phase[1]

Dr. Joshua M. Perman presented some findings drawn from the analysis of borderline character disorders in children, adolescents, and adults, as well as from the observation of severe borderline and psychotic illness in families on public welfare. In his view they demonstrated the disorganizing effects on the ego of trauma experienced in the separation-individuation phase of ego development (Mahler, 1968). He reported that the specific effect of trauma at this stage of ego development was a fixation at a primitive level of the adaptive ego functions, with consequent maladaptation of ego functioning. The specific traumata considered was the loss of the object, prolonged physical illness, and a disturbed attitude of the mother to her child.

The evolution that leads thinking, feeling, and behavior to come under the influence of the secondary process is paralleled by the development of autonomous ego functions and the reality

[1] This material was contained in a paper, "Some Remarks on Trauma: A Study of Ego Fixation," presented by Dr. Perman at the Annual Meeting of the American Psychoanalytic Association in May, 1965 as part of the Panel on "The Concept of Trauma."

principle. As this process unfolds, the mobile sexual and aggressive energies of the id are bound and utilized, thus strengthening the ego. Traumatic experiences interfere with the establishment of the dominance of the secondary process and, as Mahler (1968) has shown, such experiences can interfere with differentiation, causing a fixation at the symbiotic phase if they occur during that phase of ego development. Fixation at the symbiotic phase is fostered by overstimulation, overprotection, and overanxious mothering by symbiotic partners. Those ego functions which characteristically develop at the separation-individuation phase have their development seriously interfered with by traumata occurring at that time, and become responsible for or are part of many maladaptive ego structures.

Clinically, the results are seen in a number of ways, most importantly in the vicissitudes of an incomplete separation between self- and object representations. This lack of differentiation imparts a weakness to the ego and is responsible for a subjective sense of inadequate ego control. An individual who fails to achieve such a differentiation has difficulty establishing the source of his perceptions, remaining uncertain whether they stem from inner or outer sources. In psychoses, this uncertainty may be continuous; in borderline characters it may be pronounced only under stress. "Object comprehension" does not reach autonomy, and "as if" phenomena are frequent. These people avidly seek for their mother in the object; without her, they cannot function. They expect others to see and feel their emotions, and they are readily influenced by the emotions of others. The child who is unclear about the source of his perceptions can develop learning problems as he becomes confused, fearful, and then enraged with school activities. Away from his mother he feels helpless in the face of school work and may defend himself by clinging to infantile fantasies of omniscience and omnipotence. In that event, failure in learning may reflect a subjective sense of "ego failure," i.e., failure to attain omnipotent wishes, separation from mother, and the sense of helplessness.

A second clinical sign, according to Perman, is the profound difficulty these individuals have in tolerating anxiety. They seek immediate relief from anxiety and may go to great lengths to accomplish this. If gratification is postponed, tension and anxiety mount to the point where ego integrity is threatened. Change of any kind is feared and resisted, and they try therefore to force the object to adapt to them rather than attempting to effect a personal change. They tend to use stereotyped, repetitive activities with which they cannot permit any interference, because these ritual activities both ward off instinctual dangers when denial fails, and protect them from a feared state of helplessness.

From extensive experience with people on public assistance, who are presumably traumatized by poverty conditions in the course of their development, Perman found that many showed gross signs of retardation in both drive- and ego development. Many resist learning and have defects in ego functioning that make reality incomprehensible, that might, for example, force them to reject assistance. Because they demonstrate a failure in the ability to differentiate self- from object representations, they may prefer living in crowded quarters with inevitable constant physical contact with others, without which they tend to panic. These individuals, therefore, often oppose a move to more spacious apartments which would interfere with their intense need for constant physical, auditory, and visual contact. Similar problems based on comparable developmental difficulties can be found in patients with other backgrounds as well.

A clinical illustration concerned a 19-year-old boy who left college in his freshman year because of a homosexual panic reaction. Like his phobic mother, he was uneasy with people and had few friends. He was very passive and idealized his older brother as his father had idealized the patient's grandfather. It was significant that his grandmother had shared his bedroom. In analysis, his anxiety about using the couch indicated his fear of ego regression; therapy was experienced as being treated like a child. Very early he reported an obligatory fantasy before sleep could occur. It consisted of his watching a man undress and have an erection. In the fantasy, he feared his impulse to ruffle the man's black hair. He professed never to have masturbated. A guilty wish to exhibit, connected with his fear of mother's anger, was repeated in the transference. His father and brother were idealized, and his intolerance of any critical thoughts about them interfered with realistic perceptions of them.

He spoke of learning as a process in which the teacher is sucked dry, leaving the teacher nothing and giving the student a swelled head. His passivity was frightening to him, for it meant others could control him. Therefore, anything originating outside of himself had to be warded off. Treatment was painful because to receive explanations was tantamount to being treated as a little boy. To learn meant to become helpless and to lose his identity. He was afraid of regressing to the point where he would again feel fused with the psychic representation of the mother. There was a great deal of evidence of a prolonged symbiotic relationship with his mother in childhood, including deficiencies in perception, cognition, object comprehension, thought, and reality testing.

When, in the second year of analysis, he returned to college, he became caught up in a competitive struggle with his brother, who was ahead of him. He felt he could catch up only by becoming his brother, an impulse which, because it meant the destruction of his brother, had to be warded off. Although it made him too anxious to perceive imperfections in his family, these imperfections were expressed in his own behavior, as the result of identification. There were many examples of concrete thinking. Because he had come from his mother, he believed nothing was really his own, not even his body. As time went on in analysis, it became more difficult for him to deny certain critical observations of his family—a necessary step to his further separation and individuation. He no longer automatically followed his brother's suggestions about his studies. Soon oedipal themes emerged, accompanied by anxiety and a defensive feminine identification. He recalled that he had toyed with transvestite activities in his early teens, and when these were forbidden by his mother they were replaced by hair-messing fantasies. The confusion and uncertainty regarding his sexual identity was seen in a childhood fantasy game he recalled: of coming downstairs wearing his mother's dress and lifting the skirt to exhibit his penis to her. He was a boy-girl, and he continued to hold on to the fantasy that sexual changes could occur after birth, so that he might yet develop breasts.

His defensive use of homosexual fantasies became less available to him as treatment progressed. Accordingly, as he sensed that he was changing, he developed great anxiety. He said at times that if he changed, he would vanish, and if he didn't admit to having erections, he did not have to be himself. Impulses to masturbate emerged more openly, and as his improvement continued, he began to worry about what would happen to his mother should he fall in love. He felt that she would be rendered helpless and exposed in all of her weakness. Graduation and army service interrupted the analysis.

Discussion

This presentation emphasized the significance of the timing of a traumatic experience in relation to the instinctual phase and to the level of ego development. These observations were intended to examine the question of whether a trauma experienced in the separation-individuation phase produces permanent symptomatic effects which are seen as clinically related to separation-individuation phenomena. In general terms, is the urgent *developmental task* in progress at the time of the trauma the determinant of the clinical picture that is produced by the trauma? It seems likely that the earlier a trauma occurs, the more global and far-reaching will be its effects on the basic ego functions. Anna Freud (1965) has stressed that the most recently acquired developmental skill is the one to suffer first under emotional stress. Identification played an important role for this patient in "communicating" thoughts critical of his family, consistent with a preoedipal level of development prior to clear separation and differentiation between self- and object representations. Nonetheless, important data were missing regarding his early years, so that it was impossible to tell whether a significant trauma had occurred in the separation-individuation phase. The nature of the trauma and the specifics of the disturbed mother-child relationship were not clear. The most that could be said was that the patient's need to externalize and animate inner feelings, the evidence of deficient differentiation between self- and object representations, the specific ego deficiencies connected with learning, *might* all be connected with qualities of ego functioning at the separation-individuation phase of development.

The term "ego fixation" has not been used previously in the literature, whereas many other terms, such as fragmented ego, ego deviation, ego distortion, ego defect, ego restriction, primary disturbance of the ego, and developmentally retarded ego have been used. Perman chose this term because, in his view, ego functions develop along phase lines similar to those seen in libidinal development and may undergo fixations just as drives do. Under stress, regression can occur to these fixation points. Thus, Perman suggested, if we accept the concept of ego regression, there should logically follow a concept of ego fixation. This suggestion did not meet wide acceptance. It was felt that in contrast to the step-like progression followed by the libido in the course of development, the maturation of ego functions pursues a much less sharply phasic line. Fixation points are consequently much more difficult to delineate in the ego, and it therefore seemed that the concept of ego fixation would not be helpful or aid clarity.

Presentation 6: Early Maternal Deprivation as a Trauma

Dr. Augusta Alpert of The Child Development Center presented a therapeutic approach to children who had suffered very early and very severe trauma in the mother-child interaction.[2] Children with a history of markedly traumatic mother-child relationship constitute a severe diagnostic and therapeutic challenge, and most therapists have been largely pessimistic about the outlook for them. Dr. Alpert's presentation was of great interest because it not only contributed to a study of the effects of trauma, but also described a promising therapeutic approach. Although these children display many symptoms associated with childhood schizophrenia—withdrawal, poor reality-fantasy balance, impaired object relations—Dr. Alpert contended that a reliable diagnosis cannot be made until the modifiability of the effects of the trauma can be assessed. The use of a "corrective object relation" (COR)

[2] This material was part of an unpublished paper entitled, "Corrective Object Relations: A Review and Re-Evaluation (1953-1966)."

was an exploratory attempt to assess that modifiability. The impairment of primary object relations due to the trauma caused the seeming inability in these children to form a trusting relationship with a therapist, and consequently led to therapeutic failure. Viewed as a deficiency syndrome, the impairment of primary object relations raised for Dr. Alpert the question of restitution, rather than therapy in the conventional sense.

Taking as a clue her experience with a symbiotic boy who was able to detach himself from his mother after forming a secondary symbiotic relationship with his special teacher and who then led the teacher on a *regressive* path down the zonal scale, and *progressively* back to phase-appropriate behavior, Dr. Alpert became increasingly impressed with the therapeutic potential of regression in the service of therapeutic restitution. The regression down the zonal scale had been *actively* pursued by the patient and was spontaneously reversible; on each occasion the regression was accompanied by a manic affect and the achievement of a higher level of functioning. This seemed comparable to regression "in the service of the ego" (Kris).

Dr. Alpert presented case material on two children: the first case was studied in the COR project before skills had been sharpened by experience, the second was studied later in the program. Both cases have been reported elsewhere and will be only briefly summarized here.

Case No. 1: Carol (Alpert, 1957) was brought for help at age two years, one month, because she refused to give up the bottle, was unable to accept toilet training, and could not tolerate separation from her mother. She had, as well, a low frustration tolerance. After Carol was three months old, her mother returned to work and Carol was cared for by three grandparents. At 15 months she developed coeliac symptoms, but not until the pediatrician advised hospitalization at 21 months did the mother stay at home with her baby, after which Carol steadily improved. In the observation nursery, Carol was diagnosed as a schizoid child with disturbances in identification and object relations. More detail emerged after one year of observation. Self-identity, identification with adults and peers, reality testing, and defenses were all impaired. Autonomous ego apparatus was relatively unimpaired: perception, memory, and speech were well developed; mobility was awkward, synthetic function poor, and primary-process thinking prominent even for a two-and-a-half-year-old.

These deficiencies matched the deficiencies in mothering—although the patient had had "multiple mothering," no one object could or did meet her developmental needs. She did not achieve object constancy, but tended to split the object. She missed the experience of the object as psychic organizer (Spitz), and she missed the libidinal attachment to an object that helps the child move from phase to phase in development. Carol achieved this step only after becoming attached to one teacher, just as reported by Freud and Burlingham in *Infants without Families* (1944) and *War and Children* (1943).

After one year in the nursery, Carol showed very little gain in either ego or libidinal development. She was therefore assigned to a special teacher who was to "provide a constant, consistent, need-satisfying relationship in an attempt to make good the discontinuity of early object relations." But Carol did not respond to this exclusive relationship with libidinal regression. Her primary-process verbalization began to flow freely; and in the course of this behavior revealed a number of deficits in ego organization which Dr. Alpert believed were associated with deficits in mothering in the first two years of life. These were: deficient cathexis of mental representations, splitting of object representations, impaired differentiation between object- and self representations, impaired differentiation between animate and inanimate, and primitive identification processes. Differentiation of fantasy and reality and adaptation to reality were painfully achieved step by step by balancing gratification and frustration in treatment. Peer relationships appeared next, after a temporary decathexis of her special teacher following a frustration.

This case emphasized the importance of careful diagnostic evaluation with an eye to pinpointing the etiological factors. Dr. Alpert was not certain that multiple mothering was "the trauma" in this case, but some trauma colored the oral phase of development, as the child's passionate attachment to her bottle suggested. The bottle-as-object implies a weak libidinal attachment to the primary object. The final diagnosis was: deficiency in mothering—

specifically in the libidinal component and as psychic organizer—resulting in impairment of the capacity for identification and object relations, as well as for integration, organization, and synthesis.

Case No. 2: Greta (Alpert, 1959) was a "schizoid child with depressed mood" who appeared autistically withdrawn in the nursery. The second of five children born in a period of six and a half years, it was understandable that she was deprived of good mothering. When Greta was three months old, her mother became pregnant and gave birth at term to a son who died 12 days later. Greta was a year old at the time and weighed only 18 pounds. She had been a poor eater since the age of eight to nine weeks, when she was abruptly weaned. Because girls were unwanted in this family, the loss of the infant boy increased the mother's hostile rejection of Greta. She was a crying infant whom the mother had to carry everywhere until the age of seven months. Then her mother decided to let her cry it out and lie in her vomit, "and it worked." Greta showed a mood change at that time. She stopped crying and lay passively in her crib.

The abrupt interruption of the symbiotic relationship can be reconstructed as the acute trauma; the maternal neglect can be seen as the stress trauma. Severe disturbances in the psychobiological antecedents of introjection and projection—i.e., food intake and expulsion—influenced the prominence and the form of these mechanisms.

At age four years, four months she was assigned to COR to see whether therapeutic regression could be induced to the level of traumatic fixation and to see what restitution could accomplish. For many months, in every session she demonstrated a preoccupation with food, enacting the theme of insufficient food for the greedy, insatiable baby endangered by the bad mother who did not feed or protect. The special teacher gave her ample supplies of food, care, protection, and cuddling. In about two weeks Greta was able to invite her teacher to her home and began to admire her clothes. The teacher was not only a source of supply, but there was a beginning identification. In her play she also identified with the teacher as a protector, saving toys from imaginary dangers, usually oral in nature.

Greta's anger and frustration when the winter vacation was announced was calmed by the consolation gift of a toy cat and mouse. She was delighted, said how much she loved them, adding next day that she had fed them and there had been plenty for both. Following an exchange about the importance of eating and the process of growing bigger, Greta admired the teacher's lapel pin and said that her mother had a similar one. This indicated the inclusion of her mother in Greta's libidinal attachment to the teacher, a step in the changing image of the mother and in the patient's mood.

Following the winter interruption, Greta appeared withdrawn and deprived again, and enacted a game of starvation with the toys. When assured that there was plenty of milk, her high spirits returned. Reciprocity entered the relationship two weeks later, when she brought the teacher a piece of candy-coated chewing gum. At the same time she revealed the fantasy that sex is determined by food. Dr. Alpert used this to illustrate the distinction between COR and analysis. Whereas analysis would tend to probe and eventually interpret the fantasy, COR provides libidinal supplies, where a deficit is indicated, through the intervention of a corrective relationship.

During the next several months of treatment, anal, phallic, and oedipal interests periodically intruded. She asked to be taken to the toilet and enacted wishes to spank naughty babies for making "cocky in diapers." She fed dolls and often drank from the bottle herself, yet she also expressed a wish to be like the teacher and to have a baby, and even played at mothering a toy baby. She demonstrated a growing ability to tolerate postponement of gratification when she recognized that she was smaller than the teacher, but that was because "I'm a kid" now, but "I'll grow up to be a lady, too."

Greta later regressed to being held and cuddled, announcing that she was a baby. She took to sucking on a bottle more than ever, without evidence of guilt. In games she was the tender feeding mother and was gay and euphoric. On her birthday, she became fascinated by a bubble pipe the teacher had placed in the room and put all her toys into the soapy water. She made them babies who, on the one hand, were endangered by a robber who was going to eat them up and, on the other, were about to be saved by another toy. She abruptly ended the game, refused her usual snack (defense against cannibalistic fantasies), and then announced that she was five years old. For a short time thereafter she angrily re-established regressed cuddling and nursing play, but gradually weaned herself of it. Leaving for the summer was appropriately difficult. She helped pack the toys and parted affectionately.

In summary, Dr. Alpert stated that, although Greta initially looked like a schizophrenic child with withdrawal symptoms, preoccupation, muttering to herself, and paranoid-like rages, all these symptoms were replaced by good response to the special teacher's intervention.

Regression played an important role in these two cases, both as an exploratory and a corrective tool. Greta's acute trauma was localized in the symbiotic phase, and the oral receptive-symbiotic phase in therapy appeared to be internalized as a "corrective experience." Her capacity for object relationships improved, her mood changed from sullen depression to consistent cheer. Passivity was replaced by appropriate object-directed aggression; withdrawal was replaced by peer participation. There was steady progress from the oral-sadistic to the phallic-oedipal phase. The arrest or block in development in the conflictual sphere of ego functions was reduced by the regressive experience. In this connection, Dr. Alpert emphasized that COR can be used as a preparation for analysis, as it was in fact for both these children. It strengthens the ego, especially with regard to the process of identification—and also of object relations, without which transference neurosis is impossible. She doubted whether either of the cases presented had enough structural differentiation before COR for conflict to crystallize.

Discussion

Dr. Alpert's focus had been on localizing the trauma for therapeutic considerations. She is therefore not able from this material to correlate specific ego defects with specific traumata; nor could she relate a specific trauma to the phase of development in which it occurred or to detailed qualities of the relationship to the primary object. The regression she described as essential to the good therapeutic result is spontaneous, not planned nor induced. It is, however, an integral part of the treatment and of the resultant improvement. Dr. Alpert viewed the absence of regression as a defense against the object relationship; only a limited therapeutic result can be expected without regression.

Some doubt was expressed about whether regression to a point of fixation had occurred. The clinical data suggested the formulation that these cases had never progressed beyond a point of fixation, and in the presence of a favorable therapeutic climate they were able to express this fixation openly. Dr. Alpert agreed that this was a possible interpretation but noted that the distinction should be made between regression and the loosening of defenses. No satisfactory answer could be found as to whether the clinical picture could be described as a regression, therapeutically handled by the gratification of wishes and needs (as opposed to a psychoanalytic approach) or as a procedure involving the therapeutic uncovering of the pathology by the elimination of defenses. Whether or not regression played a central role in the process, the positive relationship with the therapist, which allowed for the development of a sense of basic trust in the object, was an essential factor in the clinical improvement. A careful study of the early histories of the children helped by COR, and of those not helped by COR, could lead to a better understanding of the factors that are important in the ability to develop a sense of basic trust.

Dr. Alpert's presentation clarified the effects of a specific trauma —that is, maternal deprivation—on a specific ego function—the ability to identify. In general, it was believed that these deprived children had undergone a global trauma, the impact of which was registered in every aspect of ego functioning, making it very difficult to pinpoint specific ego impairments caused by early maternal deprivation. This bears out the view that the earlier a trauma occurs, the more profound and global its effects. Dr. Alpert's cases also confirmed Hartmann's work concerning the interdependency of ego functioning and libidinal relationships, demonstrating that when one improved, so did the other.

Following on Dr. Alpert's presentation, the question of preventive measures was raised. It was suggested that the concept of trauma was less useful in preventive work than the concept of pathogenesis. An experience should be designated pathogenic only when there is evidence of its causal role in producing mental disorder. A preliminary and admittedly inadequate, classification of the psychogenesis of childhood psychiatric disorders, intended to provide a framework for rational preventive measures, was offered. A distinction was made between primary preventive measures, which are useful in anticipating psychopathological impact, and secondary ones, which are useful following pathological psychic impacts. The first type consisted of educating parents, in order to prevent overstimulation and deprivation of the child, and preparing in advance children who must face fear, anxiety, or conflict. The second type consisted of measures that would lead to retroactive mastery—psychoanalysis and a gamut of other techniques.

When a severe deprivation has occurred in infancy (for example, the death of mother), there may be little that can be done psychiatrically until the child is two or three years old. A good mother-substitute provided within a short period of time may prevent pathological sequelae of the object loss (as Alpert's presentation suggested). When the child is old enough to participate in therapy, technical measures aimed at releasing affective tensions which the child could not formerly discharge unaided can be utilized. Strengthening the reality-testing function is also important in such cases, lest it be overwhelmed by the wish to retain the lost parent. At a later age, conflict and anxiety can be dealt with preventively by mastery in advance, utilizing measured confrontations at a low-dosage level.

This view of the terms trauma and pathogenesis was questioned on the basis of the observation that a trauma need not produce a pathogenic result. It can, in fact, under optimal circumstances enhance a maturational push. It is also questionable whether the widespread use of preventive techniques would be as beneficial as has been suggested. There is room for spontaneous and healthy mastery of a traumatic situation without outside therapeutic intervention. It is possible, for example, for a therapeutically eager analyst to overburden a traumatized child who has suffered the death of a parent with too much awareness of his reactions to the death. There are situations in which the child would have mastered the trauma in his own fashion quite adequately had there been no "preventive" approach. Careful selection of cases for treatment is still preferable to a more general preventive approach. The latter invites the mistaken notion that the term trauma applies to that which upsets or proves to be disturbing to the analyst observer, rather than that which upsets the balance of forces at work in the individual undergoing the traumatic experience.

This subject continued to elicit interest at the plenary discussion of The Kris Study Group, held at the conclusion of the work of this section. Dr. Charles Brenner supported the view that the term "pathogenic" could not replace the term "traumatic" because a psychic trauma may further normal psychic development, and so could not be defined only by its pathogenic effects. In his view, a psychic trauma is an experience that intensifies intrapsychic conflict, the effects of which are a mixture of normal and pathological reactions, which may be short or long-lasting.

Dr. Rudolph M. Loewenstein remarked on the wide range of approaches the Group had taken to the concept of trauma, and specifically asked for clarification of the replacement of the term trauma by the concept of pathogenic experience. The discussant who had presented this latter emphasis explained that the term trauma to him had denotative and connotative qualities, and it was specifically the connotation emphasizing the external origin of trauma to which he objected. No external event could be clearly independent of prior experience in the process of producing a psychic illness, and he therefore felt the term was an incongruence in psychoanalytic thinking. He preferred the term "pathogenesis" because it was broader and included the concept of trauma; it did not connote an emphasis on the external, and it allowed for the consideration of long and short term factors. It placed stress on detectable pathology and therefore had the advantages of an operational term. Adding the term "experience" to that of "pathogenic" in his view, emphasized the significance of the inner state, with all its prior development.

CHILDHOOD TRAUMA STEMMING FROM WITHIN: ILLNESS OR PHYSICAL DEFECT AS TRAUMA

Presentation 7: A Case of Congenital Strabismus

The study of this 23-year-old girl was focused on her congenital strabismus, although it is important to note that this was neither the only trauma, nor even the major trauma, from which she suffered.[3] The case quite naturally drew attention to the significance of a long-lasting physical disability and raised the question whether such a physical ailment can be considered a psychic trauma in the usual sense of the term.

The patient came to analysis because of insomnia and the fear that an old symptom, her childhood sleepwalking, would recur. She thought of herself as psychotic (her mother was a borderline psychotic) and throughout her life had often wondered, "Who is crazy, me or my mother?" Her only sibling, a severely retarded brother seven years her senior, had an exaggerated strabismus and suffered from frequent convulsions. He shared a room with her until he was institutionalized, at the age of 13, because of his overt and uncontrolled masturbation. The brother continued to spend holidays at home, sharing the patient's bedroom until she protested forcefully when she was nine years old.

In order to avoid being asked by the state to pay for the son's hospitalization and to keep secret the fact that they had money, the family lived in a slum neighborhood next to a school for the blind. The father seemed to the patient more a feminine than a masculine figure, especially after the coronary attack he suffered when she was nine years old. He used to play games with her, which heightened the level of excitement between them until they eventually became aware of an erotic component in the games. Some of these games were "playing dead," or seeing who could outstare the other. Her mother, a sadomasochistic exhibitionist, lost no opportunity to blame the patient for her Caesarean scar, displaying it openly to her. Unable to tolerate the child's

---

[3] This material was subsequently elaborated and published (Lipton, 1970).

activity, the mother prolonged her sleeping in a crib and her confinement in a stroller, so that the patient walked the first day she was put on the ground—at 14 months. The mother reduced the patient to a state of helplessness in three important ways. First, on the slightest provocation, she gave her an enema, forcing more and more fluid into her, despite her protests, until the child collapsed, often producing a violent reflex inundation of the mother. Second, the mother's frequent prolonged and towering rages ended only when the patient was reduced to tears. Third, she delighted in tickling the patient to the point of helpless exhaustion.

Visual traumata and experiences of violence were commonplace in her childhood. There were, for example, frequent violent fights between her parents, and between her mother and maternal uncles. Primal-scene experiences were frequent, and at three years of age she witnessed a stabbing in her backyard. As a child she was on one occasion pressed against a wall in a menacing manner by a frightening Negro. Beating fantasies began at the age of seven, and at 12 or 13 she began anal masturbation, using her mother's douche nozzle.

As part of the early transference during her analysis, she saw the doctor as a phallic mother administering an enema. Although composed and competent in her daily life, in her sessions the patient regressed and behaved as a struggling child, panic stricken and angry. Four years of analysis produced marked improvement in her symptoms, in her relationship with her parents, and in her sexual adjustment. A great deal of analytic work was done on her anal perversion and her masochism. The transference became more oedipal in nature, and there was a solid therapeutic alliance. Despite this improvement, many of her analytic hours continued to be characterized by the following pattern. She would suddenly become silent, then venture a comment to elicit a response. When this failed, she had an impulse to turn on the couch and plead for the analyst to talk to her or to touch her. When this failed, she would find a way to look at him. These times were characterized by statements such as, "Things are moving strangely," or, "You're getting further away," or, "I'm going crazy." Often she felt that she had something to tell the analyst, but did not know what it was. When the analyst moved his office, and for a short time the couch faced a blank wall, she found it uncomfortable to have nothing to rest her eyes on, turning on the couch more frequently to look at the analyst. It was during this period that, in one session, she reported having two simultaneous thoughts, was in doubt about which of them to verbalize, tried to suppress one but failed, and, in panic, voiced the fear that she was losing control of her mind. The analyst recaptured from his preconscious store of recollections a once barely-mentioned fact of the patient's history, namely, that as a child she had a strabismus. He suggested that her problems in free-associating reminded him of her strabismus, with its early conflict over which visual, rather than which verbal, point to focus on. The patient immediately developed a headache and a diplopia which lasted five days. There followed a major piece of working through. It emerged that she had been analyzing with her eyes closed, and this form of "not looking" was closely connected with her general use of withholding and denial. She regarded the physiological effect of the strabismus (diplopia, tilting, distance distortions, drifting of images in front of one another) as ego-alien equivalents of psychosis. After a period of working through, she spontaneously took up ice skating and stopped saying at the end of her analytic sessions that there was something she had to tell the analyst that she could not recall. Her strabismus, it became clear, was treated in much the same way as her anal perversion—namely, as a shameful secret. It had been erotized as a child, when she enjoyed the dizziness and sense of her eyes' being out of control after rolling down hills, an activity she loved. Seeing double in her sessions gave rise to a fear that she was "going crazy," so that she needed a point to focus on; therefore, her wish for an orienting stream of words from the analyst, or for physical contact. Her eyes would "slip" when she was aroused either sexually or aggressively, with the result that she would withdraw from the situation. It meant for her that she was "sexually" bad or "cross." The visual difficulty also had adverse effects on reality testing and on superego functioning, the superego being gradually corrupted by the need to keep secret the strabismus, much as in the case of a perversion (Greenacre, 1953b, 1955) . The patient has since been able to form better relationships with men, and her self image has shown a marked improvement. She had her eyes examined and started a series of exercises which promised good results. One day she even said, "No one ever told me analysis would make me beautiful."

Discussion

The two most prominent areas of trauma in this case are the strabismus and the experiences this patient had at the hands of her psychotic mother. Neither a strabismus nor a psychotic mother could be considered traumatic in Freud's sense of the term, i.e., causing a breach in the stimulus barrier. When we speak of the trauma of having strabismus or a psychotic mother, however, we are using a shorthand way of referring to the impact of the experiences on the individual. These have to be studied and evaluated carefully. Occurring regularly and even daily, they could well constitute experiences of traumatic proportion. It is important that the strabismus occurred in a setting of multiple visual shocks, and one could regard the symptomatology as related to these shocks rather than to the strabismus. The patient's exposure to many visual shocks makes the task of isolating the specific cause-and-effect relationships involving the strabismus more difficult. Nevertheless, the therapeutic response to the interpretation of her strabismus was so specific, that it indicates a clear causal relationship. The patient's analyst agreed that conflicts other than the strabismus played a role in her symptoms, but held to the view that the strabismus was the central trauma around which the symptoms he chose to highlight were organized. In his view, the strabismus was also drawn into her many other conflicts.

The clinical material suggests that the strabismus may have had specific effects on psychic structures. The need to keep family secrets and to keep her perversion and the strabismus unknown to the world must have had an important impact on superego development. As for ego functions, external perceptions and inner states were confused, and self representation and body image were adversely affected. Perhaps the patient used the strabismus for the defensive purpose of rationalizing that her mother's "craziness" was like cross-eyes, in that it was temporary and would pass. One suggestion raised was that she might have used the strabismus as a "screen experience" or "screen trauma" to ward off an identification with her defective brother. There is a vital difference between the concrete, tangible reality of a trauma related to a body defect that is in itself unchangeable, and a transient trauma, especially one based on fantasy wishes. A quality of physical immutability is responsible for a forceful and long-lasting structuring of psychic events relating to the defect. In addition to the quality of unshakable reality, the traumatic experience of having strabismus in this case had a changeable quality. Strabismus comes and goes and yet is never completely gone.

It would not do justice to the clinical data to consider the strabismus the major trauma in this case. The traumatic effect of the psychotic mother was much more profound. Her analyst considered her major traumata to have been related to the mother's rages and the enforced enemas.

This case again demonstrated the difficulty in delineating a single trauma for study. Despite careful efforts to tease out one traumatic experience (the strabismus) and isolate it under the analytic microscope, it became clear that a number of traumatic factors were inseparably linked to it, the clustering effect of traumatic experiences. The patient's history revealed a long-standing stress trauma endured in the relationship with her mother, very likely from birth on, complicated by the stress of living closely with the disturbed exhibitionistic brother, and compounded by the emotional stress of her relationship with a seductive father. In the setting of this network of stress trauma the strabismus with which she was born became significant.

Presentation 8: The Case of a Dying Child

This case illustrates the struggle of a child suffering from leukemia in dealing with the enormous emotional strain which the knowledge of his fatal illness imposed upon him. How his parents unwittingly added to his burden and suggestions of therapeutic importance in such tragic situations emerge from the report.

Charles, four years, seven months old, came to psychiatric treatment seven months after a two-week period of hospitalization which had established the diagnosis of leukemia. Having received a sternal puncture, blood transfusion, and numerous finger punctures, he emerged from the hospital with newly-developed symptoms of daytime urinary incontinence, occasional soiling, and whining and clinging behavior. For two weeks he slept in his mother's bedroom and was unable, because of anxiety and the intensity of his symptoms, to separate from her in order to attend a nursery school. Urinary incontinence grew worse, and he tended to play more and more with girls, assuming the role of baby or mother in the game of playing house. He often wore girls' clothing during this play. His interest in music showed no signs of regression, nor did his precocious speech, and talent in drawing and painting.

Charles had two sisters, two and four years his senior. The children were witness to constant parental quarreling. When Charles was two and a half, the marriage began to disintegrate. A permanent separation was arranged when he was three, followed by a divorce, about a year later, just two weeks prior to the diagnosis of leukemia.

Charles had reason to complain about his father's marked preference for the sisters during his increasingly infrequent weekend visits. But by the time he was four, Charles had stopped complaining. His father withdraw even further from the family after the divorce, and especially following the diagnosis of leukemia. No sharing of the reasons for the marital difficulty ever took place, leaving the children confused and unclear in their understanding of the situation.

Charles's mother, a 35-year-old sad and weary woman, was generally hypertense and inclined to feel frenzied under slight pressures. She was seldom on time for appointments and spent much of her time complaining about the mechanical disrepair of her automobile. A graduate of a first-rate college, she had worked as a nursery school teacher, was now teaching science, and, while Charles's analysis got under way, started a medical technicians' course through which she hoped to contribute to leukemia research. Her motivation was both to deny and avoid experiencing

painful reactions to the reality of the child's grave illness, as well
as to pursue her narcissistic, grandiose interests.

In his initial examination, Charles was ingratiating and sur-
prisingly spontaneous in discussing his hospitalization—an experience then seven months in the past. Picking up from the facts
that the analyst was a doctor, he spoke of having a lot of fun
and watching a lot of TV when he had been in the hospital. After
some elaboration, the analyst pointed out his "opposite talk,"
whereupon Charles readily agreed it hadn't all been a good time.
Working with the mother quickly revealed the existence of parallel
distortions in the way the mother and child viewed the facts of
their daily life. Each independently, for example, used the wrong
name to identify Charles's summer school teacher, using instead
the name of someone they had hoped would be his teacher but
who, to their disappointment, was not. Similarly, Charles insisted
his pediatrician was his sister's doctor, therein identifying with
his healthy sister and taking for himself a doctor who did not
give pain and bad news.

An effort was made to undo these distortions therapeutically to
test whether Charles could make a better adaptation to the truth
than to avoidance of the truth. The mother was helped to undo
some distortions, at first peripheral ones like the teacher's name,
and later some of the grimmer facts about Charles. She was made
more aware of the effect on him of being subject to the various
hospital experiences without having had any of the procedures
explained to him. As a result of this exploration, the mother
entered therapy.

Charles's first communications in analysis dealt with pleasure
taken in aggression against himself and hinted at the possibility
that his feminine identification was related to his hospital experience. He invented devious means of retaliation when children
assaulted him. "You like trucks, I'm going to give you one, but
it'll be so rusty you can't play with it." (The emphasis was on
great temptation coupled with unrelenting frustration.) He soon
indicated some of his hopes for the future, which combined a
defensive denial with phallic strivings: "When I grow up, I'm
going to have a car." But he spoke of being scared by TV shows
about being lost in space, and by one-eyed robots. The latter

perhaps referred to his sore eyes. An alarming facial rash which he developed was dealt with in play as he enacted the role of a doctor examining what was wrong with some skin. Using clay as skin, he sliced it with a knife, studied a section, and slowly gave his opinion: "It's going to be all right." Soon, greater freedom in expressing sexual curiosity and fantasies appeared. In the third week, in enacting a fantasy play concerning little lost lambs needing protection, he expressed a fear of death for the first time. He built a fortress for them, but carefully required the windows to be open, for they could die from lack of air.

A dramatic turn in Charles's analysis occurred at this point. Ten days earlier a neighborhood dog had died, and the mother could not bear to tell her children about it. After she made a slip in the session, referring to the dog as Charles, the mother decided to "level" with her children, and told Charles about the dog five minutes before class started. On entering the class, Charles went directly to the analyst, sat down, and had his mother sit next to the analyst in the nursery schoolroom. Seriously, and with appropriate sadness, he said, "You know, Spot was sick and he died." Then he added, "You know, I'm sick, and I'm going to die." His mood was one of calm sadness. The analyst proceeded to draw him out about his illness and the dog's death. Charles gave his views of the seriousness of his illness, and the analyst offered his own. The analyst said, true, Spot had died, and it must have been a serious sickness that made Spot die. But wasn't his serious sickness a different matter? Spot was a dog, and he is a child. Spot never even went to a dog doctor or hospital. Nobody even knew Spot was sick. Spot never got dog medicine or dog blood, nor did he take dog pills every day. "It's different for you, even though you do have a serious sickness, and you might die from it, because children do die from the serious sickness you have. . . ." At no time during this statement did Charles's attention wander from the analyst.

He proceeded well in his analysis. A preoccupation with fixing broken kitchen equipment and making a magic button that could fix all broken parts for good was interpreted as his wish to get well forever by being fixed in a magical way. When the father of a classmate died he was very anxious, wanted to withdraw, and toyed with the transvestite impulses.

In the midst of his fear about his own impending death, he was also dealing with his oedipal problems and sexual confusions. He spoke of a bull called "Daddy Cow" that had a baby inside. The bull is killed and the baby lives on inside. Later the bull comes back to life. The themes of death and coming back to life were repeated several times. The confusion in sexual roles and the reversibility of death were discussed, whereupon he expressed a direct, positive, oedipal wish, telling a story in which he, in a fit of jealousy, kills the father.

Charles had developed a strong attachment to the teachers and to the analyst, and did not welcome school holidays. He made clear his view that a dead person cannot move or breathe, but added, "but he can learn." It was felt that this comment expressed the fantasy that he would continue to be with his teachers and analyst after death. He equated concerns regarding blindness with concerns about death.

By the end of two months, he no longer wet his bed, he no longer soiled, he separated easily from his mother, and went freely outdoors to play with friends. He was as creative as ever and was eager to learn from books.

Now Charles began to express directly his resentment against fate and his envy of his healthy sisters. He began to hit his mother and classmates, in contrast to the earlier verbal revenges. But at the same time, his concern for his deteriorating physical state was always in evidence.

As with the previously cited clinical examples Charles experienced a set of interrelated traumata. Living with a constant fear of death, experiencing a variety of medical procedures and interventions, the absence of the father, the withdrawal of the mother, and the possible fantasy of having succeeded in wishing his father away—with its attendant guilt reactions—are the obvious possibilities. Charles's thoughts about death had been dealt with in the therapy much as a child's thoughts about sexuality would be, that is, matters which he had observed, asked or spoken about (e.g., death of the pet) were discussed honestly. It was not considered desirable to deal with aspects of the illness and death which would be, at best, incomprehensible and, at worst, perplexing, any more than it would be helpful to talk with a child about sexual matters on levels beyond his comprehension or curiosity. Just as one would allow a child to know that sexual feelings do occur at his age, were he troubled by them, so it was considered essential to let Charles know that death can occur at his age, thus keeping the channel of communication with significant adults open for him. To this child, death meant the loss of movement, the loss of breathing, and of vision, yet he had the fantasy that in death one could continue to learn. To him death was also a reversible state. Perhaps, he conceived of death as equivalent to sleep.

Discussion

Emerging from a study of Charles's case was a concept that his analyst referred to as "pediatric dosage of reality." As with all medicine, the smallest doses are given to the smallest children, and it is desirable to dissolve the medication in a suitable vehicle, in this case a reliable human relationship.

That he wore female clothes after his illness began and that his drawings contained extra limbs suggested that Charles had a masturbatory problem which was dynamically linked to a threat of object loss and a threat to the integrity of the self representation. The transvestism in this sense represented an effort to hold onto the mother because a loss of object threatened. There very likely were associations which connected the father's abandonment of the family with the threat of loss.

A considerable amount of discussion centered around the analyst's specific interpretation, telling the child that he may die. Opinions were sharply divided about whether this was necessary or even helpful. No doubt it successfully re-established contact and communication with the important adults in his life, replacing a conspiracy of silence about his illness. The factor of death may becloud the essential principles involved, which are the same in dealing with an injured or sick child who is not in danger of losing his life. The principle to be followed is that of communicating the reality of the situation to the child and of giving adequate parental support. This was done for Charles, and as a result he no longer felt isolated and alone. The benefit to the child came from establishing a climate in which one could talk about something that had been hitherto avoided. It produced closer contact with meaningful adults in his life and counteracted the sense of object loss. One must talk about whatever is bothering a child patient, and in this case the child's foremost concern was the question of his own survival. Avoiding the issue would make him feel further isolated, and to ask him what he meant by dying, as was suggested, would be too intellectual and would probably make him feel it was impossible to talk about his worries, even with his analyst. Talking of death, in fact, was a superficial level of interchange, since it was so close to the surface of consciousness.

Another important factor involved in offering this interpretation was the belief that the analyst must at all times support the patient's reality testing. To avoid or evade Charles's awareness that he was going to die would hinder this important ego function. In this sense, the interpretation helped the child feel that he was at last understood. Countertransference and counteridentification problems have enormous potential force in treating a dying child, and much of the opposition to the procedure used, which was raised in the discussion, no doubt resulted from the mobilization of such feelings in the members of the study group.

The distinctions made by the analyst between the dog's experiences and the child's experiences can similarly be viewed from a different angle. Did it offer hope to Charles, or did it show the analyst's anxiety so that he was in danger of falsely reassuring the patient that his worries were unfounded, as the adults around the child had done all along? Toward the end of his communications with Charles, the analyst was less anxious and was able to confront Charles directly with the possibility of his dying, and it was the the direct confrontation that was the most helpful part of the communication. The analyst volunteered that he did in fact feel least happy with the earlier reassuring comments stressing that Charles was different from the dog.

Except for the initial experience of learning about a fatal illness, one cannot describe living with the knowledge and fear of impending death as a shock trauma in the usual sense. It is not a sudden, piercing, destructive stimulus, but an overwhelming, ongoing stress of great intensity that may share with the effects of shock trauma the fact that it can paralyze or render helpless, produce regressive phenomena, and deprive the ego of conflict-free energy (evidenced in loss of sublimations) and of certain autonomous functions. It produces a situation not unlike the concentration camp experiences—without the tormenting tortures from the oppressors—in that one's fragility, vulnerability, and passive helplessness before overwhelming powers is greatly enhanced. The material did not permit observations about a latency period before the appearance of traumatic effects, but neither did it rule out such a latency period.

It is noteworthy how regularly the ego, in its efforts to master the traumatic experience, resorts to identification with the aggressor. It was manifest in this case, as well as in many of the previous case reports—the concentration camp victims, the character formation of the woman who suffered an early sexual trauma (Presentation 2). The child whose father died identified with his father, and the leukemic child, at times, identified with his healthy sisters and with the doctors who carried out the medical interventions. Perhaps identification with the aggressor is a chosen mechanism of defense in traumatic situations because of the prominence of a subjective sense of helplessness in the face of overwhelming emotional forces.

A STUDY OF THE EGO'S STRUGGLE WITH A PSYCHIC TRAUMA SEEN IN *STATU NASCENDI*

The following clinical material comes from the discipline of psychoanalytic observation of children, rather than from the psychoanalytic treatment of a child patient.[4] It was included in this study because it carefully documented the ego's prolonged struggle to master a traumatic impact while that struggle was unfolding. This presentation also raises important theoretical questions and speculations about the theory of castration anxiety insofar as the specific trauma under study—the discovery of the difference between sexes—occurred long before the phallic phase of libidinal

---

[4] This case was subsequently elaborated and published (Roiphe, 1968).

development, the period during which such traumata are ordinarily expected to occur.

Presentation 9: An Early Castration Reaction

Kate was observed daily during the second year of her life. At
the age of 19 months, following her observation of an age-mate's
exposed penis, she developed a severe castration reaction lasting
for several months. The intimate knowledge of her development,
the early age of incidence of the castration reaction, as well as
the relatively detailed observation of the vicissitudes of the reaction, made this a rewarding case study.

Kate was described as very attractive, in the newborn period,
an alert, good-tempered baby who rarely cried. Her development
during the first year was unremarkable except for its general
precocity and good quality. Kate was first seen when she had just
turned 13 months. The energy and vigor of this friendly, pretty
little child's activity were a joy to watch. She would alternate
between long periods of concentrated and precocious play with
toys and a curious exploration of the entire playroom.

When Kate was 15 months old, her father, who had been in the
army for some three months and visiting with his family only on
weekends, was sent to Europe. She promptly developed a sleep
disturbance of moderately severe proportions. She would wake,
scream and thrash about for some 15 minutes, and her quite
capable mother was unable to comfort her. The mother had
the impression that Kate was not entirely awake and did not seem
to recognize her. Her very approach, touch, and holding seemed
in itself to exacerbate the child's frantic state. Her behavior, as
observed in the nursery, deteriorated markedly over this period.
She began to fall much more frequently than usual, running to
her mother for comfort. Her approach to adults, which had been
spontaneous and easy and tended naturally to elicit a response,
now seemed almost like a caricature of what it had been. The
smile, the facial expression, began to take on the character of a
grimace. The earlier confident expectation of her ability to win
a warm response from others was altered to an almost desperate
appeal for attention. Kate had before been capable of spending
relatively long periods moving about in the nursery, exploring

or playing with toys, without having to hover or return frequently to her mother; her activity now was concentrated much more around the mother's section. After three weeks, the sleep disturbance receded, as did most of its behavioral concomitants. One of the developments of this period that did persist was a marked proclivity for Kate to stand quietly and take in visually the activity of others, a prominent characteristic in the mother but not heretofore very noticeable in the child.

When Kate was 19 months old, the acute traumatic castration reaction developed. One day while the mother was out shopping, Kate spent the afternoon at the home of one of the little boys from the nursery. He had been walking around without any clothes on, and sometime in the late afternoon they were bathed together. Later that evening she mentioned to her mother that the boy did not have any clothes on, and made particular reference to his penis. She seemed compelled to talk about the afternoon's experience, but the more she talked about it the fewer were the direct references to the penis. Ultimately she said the little boy had three "belly buttons," and a birthmark. It should be noted that she had a protruberant umbilicus and a birthmark on her hip, neither of which the little boy had.

Beginning the morning following the exposure experience, Kate, who had developed good toilet control, had numerous bowel and bladder accidents. Her mother, while troubled by the child's obvious disturbance, reacted relatively mildly to her incontinence This regression lasted for about two weeks, after which she regained control. However, for many weeks thereafter she showed an unusual mild anxiety to the flush of the toilet.

Over this same period Kate became intensely negativistic toward her mother and refused to comply with her most rudimentary requests, such as dressing and bathing, although she had previously been a cheerful, easy, good-tempered child. The negativism largely receded as toilet control was re-established. There then followed two weeks of some moderate sleep disturbance, which also soon passed.

Her mother then reported that Kate seemed contented and self-contained, able to occupy herself at home for long periods of time in wholesome and constructive play. This contrasted with what was observed in the nursery, at this same period: Kate was irritable and very frequently broke into tears, usually when some child interfered with her activity. In the setting of her intense castration reaction, she was singularly unable to tolerate such interferences and, in despair, cried helplessly. Earlier, when faced with a similar situation, she had coped with it by either asserting her own interests or shifting to some other activity without any great disturbance.

During this same period, Kate developed a very persistent and widespread speech pattern emphasizing the idea, "Something just like I have," "Suzy has a dress just like mine," and so on, endlessly. This speech pattern apparently started during the period of negativism, when her mother found it almost impossible to get through even the simplest operations. One day, while struggling to get Kate's sneakers on, she said they were just like Barbara's, a somewhat older and much admired child with whom Kate often played. Kate, seemingly intrigued with this idea readily allowed her mother to put her sneakers on. The appeal of the mother's remark undoubtedly rested on its succinct verbalization of Kate's own magical identification or defensive displacement or denial when she saw the little boy's penis. After the initial shock on observing a sexual difference, she no longer referred directly to his penis, but rather responded with the more comforting thought that he had something just like she had when she spoke of his three belly buttons and his birthmark.

One day at home, Kate was playing with crayons and deliberately broke a huge brown crayon in two. This was unusual behavior for her, since she had shown little tendency to be destructive with her playthings. After she had broken it, she tried to put it together again. When she found that this was impossible, she sobbed uncontrollably for 45 minutes, in spite of her mother's efforts to comfort her. It required very little inference to see here the child's effort to repair the narcissistic injury consequent to the passive confrontation with her castration. The intense sobbing began when it came home to her that she could not in this way hope to undo the observation of the anatomic difference between boys and girls. It is not altogether unlikely that the play signaled a fantasy of a stool-phallus equation. In any case, there was ample evidence of the fantasy wish to have a penis at this time. The mother observed the child numerous times walking about holding some object between her legs.

Some two months after the initial castration reaction, Kate began to show a striking shift in her response to situations in which other children interfered with her activity. Whereas earlier she collapsed in helpless crying, she now began to turn on the other children in furious attack. Sometimes she hit the other child, but more often she pulled the other child's hair. The hair-pulling may well be related to a sequence of events arising during the period of acute negativism. When Kate showed considerable resistance to being bathed and having her hair washed, her mother got into the shower with her. Under these circumstances, she readily complied and allowed her mother to wash her hair. She grabbed at the mother's pubic hair and made an effort to explore her genitals. Her repeated efforts, following this, to look under the skirt of adult women suggest the child's uncertainty about the existence of a hidden penis.

It may be well to summarize the vicissitudes of the traumatic reaction itself. The stunning effect of the experience, lasting for several hours, was reflected by the simple repetitive recounting of it without elaboration or distortion or, for that matter, without apparent affective response. During this time the child seemed unable to mobilize any comprehensive reactions or defenses and seemed to be fixed on establishing the primal reality of the perception. Only after several hours were organized reactions mobilized, a process which continued with remarkable elaboration for several months. The first organized reaction, unstable as it was, involved a defensive denial and displacement of the perception. This denial reflected the fundamental threat the noxious perception posed for the integrity of the self representation. The denial was incapable of containing the disruptive traumatic force of the experience and, within less than 24 hours, resulted in impressive regressive reactions. What was striking within less than 24 hours after the traumatic experience was the massiveness and pervasiveness of the reactions mobilized. For several hours there was only the stunned and consequently nonreactive state

of the child. This was followed by major shifts in her aggressive
and libidinal position, as well as indications of a widespread involvement of major segments of the ego's functioning. What was
noteworthy about the reactions in this early phase was the essential passivity and helplessness they reflected. Relatively uncom-
plicated by inappropriate responses of the mother, the child began
to display more and more active reparative processes. Two
months later, the balance of the fantasies and behavior were much
more on the active side, in contrast to the earlier helplessness and
passivity.

The youngster at 15 months of age had suffered the loss of
her father and had had a typical and moderately severe separation reaction. Whereas this was precipitated by the father's leaving, it was felt to be particularly disruptive because it confronted
the child with the threat of the loss of the more highly invested
maternal object. The separation reaction was largely mastered
within a three-week period. The only noticeable precipitates of the
separation experience indicative of a lasting strain effect were a
new voracity of appetite and an identification with a characteristic tendency of her shy mother to sit quietly on the edge of the
nursery (where she took in visually the gratifying activity of her
child).

Some four months later, when the child was confronted with
the sexual difference, she manifested a profound castration reaction with developing penis envy. It was felt that the earlier separation reaction, while partially mastered at the time, had served
to sensitize this child to experiences of loss. When she observed
the sexual difference, a special kind of loss, she showed an intense
traumatic castration reaction of prolonged duration.

Discussion

The analyst who had studied Kate explained that, from this
and other clinical material, he had hypothesized a regularly occurring early genital phase in the middle of the second year of life.
Working with pseudo-autistic children, he had found that, when
they develop bowel and bladder control, there was a tendency for
a spread of the sphincter excitation to the genitals. He postulated
that a similar reaction may appear generally at the period of

toilet training, although much less intensely than in the case presented. Kate illustrated the reaction in a severe form in a nonpsychotic child. He emphasized that the castration reaction which developed during this early genital phase had no true oedipal elaboration, but instead had primarily narcissistic content organized around questions of self- and object representations. Normally this early genital phase is passed through smoothly; only with traumatic conditions such as object loss or bodily injury or illness does it become a prominent problem.

The question would then follow whether it was a fear of the loss of the object rather than castration anxiety that was being observed. But Kate's intense reaction to losing her father had subsided much earlier, and it was immediately following the exposure to the little boy's penis that she developed the specific castration reaction, including the condensation, displacement, and projection involved in describing the boy as having three belly buttons and a birthmark. One could predict a strong reaction to the loss of the father because it is seen almost universally. Far more unusual is the occurrence of such a strong and clear-cut castration reaction following exposure to the sight of a boy's genital at so young an age. The loss of the father was believed to have a genetic relation to the castration reaction, but cannot by itself account for the clinical manifestations.

There is more uncertainty when we consider whether Kate's general precocity might also include a precocious oedipal development. Greenacre has said that a preoedipal trauma leads to the persistence of the traumatic effect into the oedipal phase, which will then display the coloring of the preoedipal trauma. To help distinguish between the possibilities of a precocious oedipal development and the postulated early genital phase, it is important to know the fantasies accompanying the child's sexual excitation. There were no available data in this area, but the observers strongly suspected from the details of the castration reaction that the excitation carried with it content dealing with the body self and the distinction between self- and object representations. Saying, for example, "I have something just like someone else," served to deny the narcissistic injury consequent to the observation of the genital difference. When she was able to say later, while looking at an airplane one evening, that its blinking lights were like the stars in the sky, the content had lost its narcissistic foundation.

In attempting to account for the puzzling intensity of Kate's castration reaction, it is possible to postulate that it had its origin in the concomitant occurrence of two factors. The first is the development of genital sensitivity during the stage of ego development when the establishment of representation of the primary object and of the self is in the foreground. Secondly, at the same time some significant object loss or illness or body injury, etc., occurs. Roiphe believed that the data demonstrated an early genital phase in the case of Kate, and it seemed valuable to pursue this study to validate the proposition that this early genital phase in the second year of life is a universally occurring phenomenon in libidinal development.

Some of the now familiar factors that have been noted in previous chapters can be seen in this case report as well. There is a significant prehistory—the separation from the father and the change in the emotional climate of the family which followed, something which must have colored the child's reaction to the discovery of the sexual difference. Thus, the clustering of traumata holds true for this case too. Worthy of special attention, however, is the child's initial passivity and helplessness in the face of traumatic experience, followed only later by an active and aggressive reaction—for example, in her furious attack on chil-. dren who interfered with her activities. One can see in the latter reaction an identification with the aggressor. But the initial passive helplessness, which early on coincided with an absence of ego activity in working over or distorting the traumatic experience for defensive purposes, is evidence of a latency period which follows the trauma, prior to the development of symptomatic effects. In this case it was brief, and one could speculate it was due to a stunning effect on the ego's capacities, producing a temporary paralysis of ego functions. As a result, she repetitively related, without distortion and without affect, the experience of bathing with the little boy. The distortions of displacement and denial began to appear as the ego recovered its functional capacities, and only then were the results of defensive activity visible.

These findings were discussed further at the plenary session of the Kris Study Group. The question was raised as to what made the sight of a boy's penis traumatic to this girl, inasmuch as she was described as a normal child of a healthy, well-intentioned mother, and it is known that many girls are exposed to the sight of a penis. In response, it was noted that castration reactions in the prephallic period are not so uncommon, although few have been reported in the literature. (Anna Freud reported some instances of penis envy in children of this age group who were removed from their parents during the war.) Four months earlier, the child had experienced a separation from her father, which, it was believed, predisposed her to further trauma. The later castration reaction to the sight of a boy's penis was a reverberation of the earlier experience of loss when the father left. Dr. David Beres concurred in the belief that the period when bowel and bladder control is being established is one of increased genital sensitivity. Given certain precipitating experiences, this may predispose the child to castration anxiety at this early, prephallic level of development. Dr. Elizabeth Geleerd, in support of the observation, reported that in her early experience as an observer in Anna Freud's nursery in Vienna, she saw a little girl about 16 months old, from a good home with devoted parents, who, on being examined by the pediatrician, played with his stethoscope and put it on her genital, saying, "I hurt." This occurred during the preoedipal period.

If the child's castration reaction was a reverberation of the earlier loss when the father left the home, the question arose whether there were any precipitates of the earlier loss contained in the castration reaction. Here, only indirect evidence was available. After the father left, Kate spontaneously and without maternal encouragement, developed consistent bowel and bladder control. This might have been an attempt to hold onto the lost object. With the castration reaction, there was a temporary loss of bowel and bladder control, suggesting a relationship between the two. Secondly, it was pointed out that the child showed an identification with her mother after the father left, a tendency that was reinforced with the castration reaction.

Dr. Jacob Arlow wondered if we were justified in calling this experience, resulting in a castration reaction at 19 months of age, a trauma, as opposed to viewing it as a disturbing reaction in childhood. After some discussion, it was agreed that it would be justifiable to call the experience traumatic only after a retrospective study had revealed a lasting effect on character or symptom development. What had been demonstrated was the major organizing effect the experience had on this child, and if this influence continued to play a major role in her psychic life, it would be adequate evidence that a trauma had occurred. Therefore, only a partial answer had been provided to this question at the time the case was reported.

THE INFLUENCE OF CULTURE ON TRAUMA

Periodically during the course of discussion in this study group, questions arose relating to cultural differences in experiencing and coping with trauma. Primal-scene experiences are very prominent among the children of many areas of the world, for example, and it would be instructive to know whether or not they are traumatic in all cultures and, if not, what cultural influences account for the differences. As part of this aspect of our study, Dr. Werner Muensterberger was invited to present a preliminary draft of a paper on psyche and culture.

Presentation 10: Culture and Trauma

Dr. Muensterberger recalled that Freud, in *Totem and Taboo* (1913), had described primitive man as uninhibited, only to change his views 10 years later when he said (1923) that the differentiation of ego and id is basically similar for man regardless of sociocultural background. Primitive people have a coherent organization of mental functioning and, therefore, secondary-process structuralization. They have conflicts similar to those of modern man, although their resolution may follow different pathways. But in any social organism, primitive or civilized, man must submit to internal and external controls.

The facts that the duration of postnatal growth is 27 times that of prenatal growth, and that one-fifth to one-quarter of life has elapsed when man reaches genital maturity (other mammals reach this point much earlier) are fundamental aspects of the human condition. Similarly, the human baby depends on sucking for a much longer period than even the higher apes, producing a special period for the interplay of congenital, maturational, and environmental pressures.

Muensterberger described the method of many anthropological studies as one of sampling cultural stereotypes, disregarding variations, and making an implicit assumption that the people of a culture in general have a homogeneous reaction pattern. Man living in an associative community has had to exert self-control and achieve adaptive behavior. No preliterate people exists which condones uninhibited action. Therefore, regardless of the degree of primitivity of a culture, the human child is always born into a social organism that fosters some degree of differentiation of the "I" from the "non-I." The more primitive the culture, the stricter the organization, for it is the powerful communal bonds of primitive people that precede and function like the internalized controls of civilized man, which we call superego. The trail from Neolithic man to the Bronze and Iron Age is marked by great technological advances as well as a strong trend toward increased abstraction, differentiation of affects, and eventually an increase in self-observation and ego autonomy.

Our present knowledge tells us that a religious ritual (e.g., a sacrifice) may derive from primary-process thinking, from magical omnipotent wishes, and a desire to influence the future. But it is also a way of regulating drive activity and of effectuating restraint, sublimation, and adaptive behavior. What, then, constitutes primitivity? Muensterberger approached this question by first citing two statements of Hartmann, Kris, and Loewenstein (1951). The first notes that the ability for higher mental functions depends on the distance of ego activities from conflict, i.e., their autonomy. The second states that the increase in ego autonomy in Western man is paralleled by the internalization of aggression, which in turn contributes to superego development. Accordingly, Muensterberger suggested that primitivity refers to the fact that instinct controls depend on external or externalized agencies (projections of ghosts, demons, etc.) rather than on agencies that are internal. In religious and social taboos, moral demands are only partially internalized, so that a sociopsychological frame of reference is put at the disposal of the ego, which then operates in terms of mutual identification, while the potential for autonomous functioning is surrendered to the requirements of the group. Environment directs the defenses of primitive man more than it does those of civilized man. The group and its collective regulations take over the function of the control systems.

Typically in preliterate societies, the primitive mother devotes herself exclusively to her child for an average of two to three years. This involves breast feeding on demand and constant skin-to-skin contact as the child is carried about against her body, stimulating tactile, thermal, and kinesthetic sensations. It also includes the mother's acceptance of the child's freely urinating and defecating on her body. Thus, the differentiation of inside from outside does not develop along the same lines as in Western civilization, nor to the same degree. Also, the stimulation of body pleasure stresses narcissism and postpones ego-id differentiation and instinct-restraining development. Breast feeding in these societies is accompanied by a lactation taboo—that is, sexual abstinence. The young mother has to refuse her husband for two to three years. Some believe breaking of the lactation taboo produces illness in the child. Although psychoanalytic data are impossible to obtain in these situations, observations suggest that the experiences of nursing and cutaneous stimulation have important sexual and phallic implications. Muensterberger also said that after the breast disappears, tactile sensations immediately compensate the child for the loss, making it unnecessary to hallucinate the breast in order to restore a perceptual identity. From this, one would expect variations in the phenomenology of separation anxiety, the significance of object loss, and castration fear. He believed that this prolonged anaclitic type of dependence, which goes far beyond physiological need, fosters a social organization in primitive societies with cohesive bonds of a rigidly integrated type.

He then questioned whether there is a correspondence between this prolonged attachment to the mother and certain effects on ego and superego organization. The lactation taboo, he suggested, fosters a shift in the mother's cathexis from the husband to the child, who then unconsciously fulfills erotic needs. The equation child-phallus is probably expressed in this bond. Also, the immediacy of gratification for the child removes the impetus for hallucinatory image formation, the development of mental representations, the search and demand for transitional objects, secondary-process thinking, and the differentiation of inside and outside. We would expect blurring between inner and outer, self and non-self, and a narcissistic, projective world image. Thus, it seems that drive organization, patterns of discharge, perception, reality testing, identifications, and frustration tolerance are deeply affected. Renunciation of instinctual demands arrives relatively late in life. Separation-individuation is timed and structured differently. The ability to be alone is far more limited. The accepting and nonpunitive attitude regarding early elimination without regulatory measures permits greater tolerance for ambivalence without guilt, adds to the belief in the magic power of one's body, and allows for assimilation of anal sadistic impulses with less conflict.

The dependence on external agencies rather than internal controls limits the range and plasticity of responses and also restricts the freedom to dissociate from one's social milieu. In this can be recognized an adaptive attempt to fit into one's society, but also an attempt to secure a conflict-free relationship with the external representative of an introjected model. In other words, ancestor worship is a projective manifestation of preoedipal and oedipal conflicts. This point was illustrated with the example of a Nigerian native who had been educated in the West and then refused to comply with his family's expectations that he would return and marry the girl his parents had chosen. He explained that Western education made for little understanding between himself and his people. He added that he did not like to go home because "at night there are too many witches in the trees."

One would also like to be able to evaluate how adequately the individual members of the primitive society are sheltered by the group, its codes and patterns of behavior. Cross-cultural studies demonstrate a relationship between detribalization and the breakdown of the sociocultural order, on the one hand, and the development of sociopathic and psychiatric disorders, on the other. Socially and culturally disintegrated communities have a higher concentration of psychiatric disorders. This, too, suggests a restricted development of ego autonomy in primitive societies.

The considerations regarding the prolonged mother-child relationship suggest that in primitive man we are dealing with a fluctuation between primary- and secondary-process thinking. The ego retains a higher degree of narcissistic cathexis, part of which reinforces the solidarity of the community as the early attachment to the mother is displaced onto the group. "Primary objectless anxiety" does not seem to exist, but the child cannot forego immediate gratification. Homesickness, depression, and feelings of abandonment occur as soon as the primitive adult is separated from his familiar environment. The transition from dependence to independence, from dual unity to individuation, is never completed, in Muensterberger's view. But there are differences between this situation and the psychic functioning of the infant. Here, ideas of grandeur, omnipotence, and belief in magic exist side by side with reality-syntonic action. The emergence of object relationships, ego identifications, ideational development, etc., follow a schedule different from the one we are accustomed to. Object relationships particularly bear an oral stamp, and the apparent object hunger is related to the dread of being left alone.

Muensterberger concluded that the prolonged exclusive mother-child relationship in primitive peoples has lasting significant effects on thought processes, ego and superego development, the management of drives, and on secondary autonomy.

Discussion

Dr. David Beres focused the discussion on the question most important to our study group: Are events we consider traumatic in our culture necessarily traumatic in another culture? Dr. Muensterberger did not doubt that what was traumatic in one culture was not necessarily traumatic in another. He made it clear that one great difficulty in a study of this sort was the lack of psychoanalytic data. Information is collected through single, or occasionally, a few interviews with individuals in the primitive society. Asked if this limitation could not be compensated for by observation of adolescents and young adults with reference to the prolonged nursing and sudden weaning, he agreed that it could, but added that the connections made are in the mind of the observer because there is a lack of analytic material. He was impressed by primitive people's reaction to death, whether of a parent, spouse, or child. The lost object is rapidly replaced after 10 days to two weeks of mourning, and quickly forgotten. The cathexis is quite fluid and easily shifted to another love object.

Dr. Oscar Sachs pointed out that some Rhodesian natives with similar experiences of prolonged nursing and sudden weaning, have enormous tolerance for being alone. They have been known to walk alone as much as a thousand miles to get a job. This suggested, he believed, that, behind the tolerance for being alone seen in some of these people, there are other factors at work. Their undue optimism may be related to the prolonged nursing experience. Dr. Beres raised a question about the latter point, suggesting that the optimism may well be related to the prominence of magic and animism.

Dr. Muensterberger described weaning, which occurs between the ages of four and five, as very sudden. The child is abruptly moved from being exclusively with his mother to being exclusively with a group of peers, where new identification with nonparental objects becomes possible. A new institution, that of the best friend, develops, which he considers an example of fusion. In some tribes, friends even exchange names.

Does a boy's viewing of a female genital in these cultures often have a traumatic effect as it does in ours? The experience is almost ubiquitous in primitive peoples, and, according to Muensterberger, it always has great emotional impact. Castration fears, for example, are very intense and on the surface. Latency children imitate coitus, he believes, as a device to ward off anxiety. There is great emphasis on denial of the anatomical difference between the sexes, and the female phallus is frequently replaced by fetishistic objects. But he emphasized again the impossibility of getting any information directly from these primitive people about their sexual lives and fantasies.

Dr. David Milrod drew attention to the inability of these people to develop their object relationships to the stage of object constancy. This was seen to be confirmed by the ease with which they forgot the lost love object and substituted a new love object in its place. There seemed to be a major limitation in building a stable, differentiated, object representation as part of the psychic structure. When we consider that this process depends on introjection mechanisms and fantasies of incorporation, and that these primitive societies are so highly orally oriented, we might suspect a significant conflict in the area of oral incorporation. It was also striking, he felt, that there was a total absence in Muensterberger's paper of any material relating to oral aggression or oral aggressive fantasies. Could the oral incorporative conflict deal therefore with oral aggressive fantasies? Could it be traced to a psychic trauma, to orally colored primal-scene experiences, for example, or to cannibalistic fantasies?

The question was also raised whether clinical depressions occurred in primitive peoples, for these would possibly provide indirect evidence of an introjected object. In response, Dr. Sachs said that, in his experience, depression usually appeared when a member of a tribal society entered a Western oriented community, thus losing tribal support for the projection, which seems to ward off depressive affect and anxiety.

When asked whether the anxiety observed was largely the result of external danger or was caused by internal conflict, Muensterberger stated that by and large it was determined externally and was promoted by the culture. Nevertheless, internal conflict does contribute to some extent to anxiety through the mechanism of identification and imitation. With regard to moral imperatives, it was noted that in primitive societies very little guilt is observable, but shame reactions are prevalent. This suggests minimal mature superego development and a preponderance of superego precursors in the psychic apparatus. Prohibitions arise out of the tribal culture, which puts moral and inhibitory pressure on the individual.

Interesting as these cultural data are, they do not lend themselves to definitive statements on whether such experiences as the discovery of the sexual difference or the primal-scene experiences are traumatic in all societies. The absence of analytic data, resulting from the fact that members of primitive societies do not enter analysis or even lend themselves to analytic interviews, is the main obstacle to making meaningful comparisons between the primitive and modern culture. Muensterberger concludes, for example, that the imitation of coital movements by children in primitive societies is an expression of castration anxiety. Others have, from the same observations, arrived at an opposite conclusion. Lacking analytic data about thoughts, feelings, conflicts, and the like, such questions cannot be conclusively resolved.

SUMMARY

On May 23, 1967, a summary of the work of the study group was presented for discussion before the entire four sections of the Kris Study Group. The Chairman, Dr. David Beres, noted that because our goal had been one of allowing our clinical material to lead us to theoretical constructions, rather than working with a theoretical formulation in mind, no attempt had been made at the start to define psychic trauma in a precise way. An experience can be considered traumatic in a true sense only in retrospect, i.e., once it has produced a lasting effect on symptom or character formation. The observer's judgment or empathy is not a gauge to measure trauma; only the specific meaning the experience has for the individual can decide that question. Anna Freud and Robert Waelder both stress that it is what is traumatic to the patient that is important, thereby implying how easily one can be misled by one's own empathic reactions.

From the outset of the plenary discussion, much interest was evidenced in the problem of the definition of the term trauma, as well as in the distinctions between shock trauma and stress (or strain) trauma. Opinions ranged widely from criticism of the fact that a specific definition had been avoided to an opinion shared by many that the study group had been operating with a working definition all along, although not specifically enunciated. As in the literature, there was a difference among the discussants about the concept of shock trauma versus strain (stress) trauma. Some believed, along with Anna Freud and Waelder, that a disturbed mother-child relationship should not be considered a trauma, whereas others accepted the concept of strain trauma as it has been described by Ernst Kris. An important question was raised about differences in the course of an analysis of people

traumatized by an acute, overwhelming shock trauma, as opposed
to the analysis of people affected by a chronic stress situation. The
study group had not been able to answer the implicit questions of
whether the impact of a shock trauma differs from a strain trauma
in terms of the psychopathology produced. It was clear that a
shock trauma never occurred in a neutral setting, but was always
accompanied by other traumata and, in our experience, had a
significant prehistory of strain trauma. Although some of our
material suggested that stress (or strain) trauma affected the development of ego functions, and shock trauma affected object
relationships, we were not in a position to claim this as a general
proposition.

Dr. George H. Pollock, the Director of Research at the Chicago
Institute for Psychoanalysis, a visiting guest, enriched the discussion by sharing information about his own research experience.
He and several colleagues in Chicago were working on the same
subject, and had encountered similar difficulties. He believed it
added to clarity if the term stress was used as the stimulus, and
strain as the response, which need not necessarily be pathological.
It follows then that strain trauma may be acute or chronic, reversible or irreversible. His group dealt with a traumatic situation
along the lines of what they called the three P's—predisposition,
precipitation, and perpetuation. There may be certain predis-
posing factors present, not in and of themselves traumatic. There
may then occur minor precipitants capable of catalyzing a response, and should the child be constantly exposed to the situation,
it may be perpetuated, producing a chronic situation of trauma
that may become pathogenic. Masud Khan's (1963) concept of
cumulative trauma has been very helpful in conceptualizing
this. In addition Sandler's (1967) concept of retrospective trauma
(an event having no observable effect at the time of occurrence,
but retrospectively seen as traumatic) has been very useful to their
group in the study of anniversary reactions, for example, and other
experiences of childhood loss.

Dr. Pollock noted that the group's discussion of prevention
implied prediction, that is, relating presumably traumatic experiences to later pathology. In examining the possibility that certain
childhood experiences can be predicted to have a pathological

effect the group in Chicago has studied a number of patients who developed thyrotoxicosis following a sudden shock situation. In many, there had been significant pathology in the mother-child relationship at a time, they believe, that can be equated with the period of consolidation of the stimulus barrier. In some cases it was clear that the mother did not adequately protect the child in situations of danger, so that the child could not develop a sense of safety in the face of danger. He stressed that there was a great deal in our theoretical knowledge and empirical experience that allowed us to make probability predictions, and disagreed with those who said that we cannot predict. He cited as an example a blind prediction his group made in a study of peptic ulcers in twins, where the circumstances which they predicted would be necessary and sufficient to precipitate an ulcer, fortuitously occurred months after the prediction, and an ulcer did develop.

In the subsequent discussion, it was clarified that our use of stress (or strain) trauma had been different from Dr. Pollock's, since we had used them synonymously. Masud Khan's use of the term cumulative trauma was clarified as referring to repeated traumatic impacts brought to bear on a child, resulting specifically from a failure in the mother's function as a protective shield for the child.

It was Dr. George Wiedeman who most succinctly expressed the majority view when he underscored what in his opinion was the important central point emerging from this study: that a traumatic experience could only be understood in terms of the whole context of the individual's previous history and his ego and libidinal development at the time of the experience.

Although the conclusions to be drawn from the study are modest, there are several that merit attention. First, traumata do not occur singly, but in clusters. There are many facets to a single trauma, and there is always an important prehistory to the traumatic experience, which has an important bearing on the meaning and impact of that experience. A shock trauma often occurs in a setting of ongoing, well-established stress (or strain) trauma, and this often exists in the parent-child relationship. The shock and stress traumata are usually interrelated, the latter often forming part of the significant prehistory to the former. There was an impression that by fostering the development of inflexible defenses, stress trauma increases the individual's vulnerability to shock trauma. Similarly, suggestions that strain trauma tends to affect character formation, while shock trauma affects symptom formation, did emerge from the study, although not in a convincing enough pattern to warrant a definite formulation.

The data studied strongly support the view that an individual's reaction to a trauma depends on the phase of libidinal development and the level of ego development achieved at the time of the trauma. Other important elements affecting the reaction are the previous history of the individual and, in the case of children, the reaction of the mother to the experience.

Consistently one can find a latency period between the time of a traumatic event, and the appearance of some psychopathological effect. This may be brief, as in the case of Kate (Presentation 9), or prolonged into months and years, as in the case of survivors of concentration camps. The meaning of the latency period is not clear, although there are strong suggestions that it is related to the time taken by the ego to recover sufficiently from the disrupting impact of the trauma to institute defensive measures.

Another specific observation deals with identifications. The material studied suggests that there is a strong preference for the use of the defense mechanism of identification with the aggressor in cases of trauma. The presentations concerning the survivor syndrome, the case of an early sexual trauma, the boy whose father died, the leukemic child, and the child with an early castration reaction, all demonstrated this defense. The helplessness induced by a traumatic experience may well be related to this preference. In addition, the presentations of Drs. Kris and Solnit, and of Dr. Alpert, both demonstrated specific disturbances in the process of identification which had serious consequences in hampering further ego development. Whether traumatic experiences may play a special role in affecting the identification process or whether this relationship is only apparent because most traumata occur in childhood when the ego is weak and psychic structure is being formed, in part by identification processes, must for now remain an open question.

BIBLIOGRAPHY

Abraham, K. (1913), Mental Aftereffects Produced in a Nine-Year-Old Child by the Observation of Sexual Intercourse Between Her Parents. In: *Selected Papers on Psychoanalysis.* New York: Basic Books, pp. 164-168.

Alpert, A. (1957), A Special Therapeutic Technique for Certain Developmental Disorders in Prelatency Children. *Amer. J. Orthopsychiatry,* 27:256-269.

—— (1959) Reversibility of Pathological Fixations Associated with Maternal Deprivation in Infancy. *The Psychoanalytic Study of the Child,* 14:169-185. New York: International Universities Press.

Beck, A. T., Sethi, E. B., & Tuthill, R. W. (1963), Childhood Bereavement and Adult Depression. *Archives of General Psychiatry,* 9:295-302.

Bender, L. (1954), Children's Reactions to Death of a Parent. In: *A Dynamic Psychopathology of Childhood.* Springfield: Charles C Thomas, pp. 172-195.

Beres, D. (1956), Ego Deviation and the Concept of Schizophrenia. *The Psychoanalytic Study of the Child,* 11:164-235. New York: International Universities Press.

—— (1958), Vicissitudes of Superego Functions and Superego Precursors in Childhood. *The Psychoanalytic Study of the Child,* 13:324-351. New York: International Universities Press.

—— (1965), Ego Disturbances Associated with Early Deprivation. *J. Amer. Academy Child Psychiatry,* 4:188-205.

—— & Obers, S. J. (1950), The Effects of Extreme Deprivation in Infancy on Psychic Structure in Adolescence. *The Psychoanalytic Study of the Child,* 5:212-235. New York: International Universities Press.

Bergen, M. E. (1958), The Effect of Severe Trauma on a Four-Year-Old Child. *The Psychoanalytic Study of the Child,* 13:407-429. New York: International Universities Press.

Bergmann, T. (1945), Observations of Children's Reactions to Motor Restraint. *Nervous Child,* 4:318-329.

Bonaparte, M. (1939), *Five Copy Books.* London: Imago, 1950-1954.

Breuer, J. & Freud, S. (1893), On the Psychical Mechanisms of Hysterical Phenomena. *Standard Edition,* 2:3-17. London: Hogarth Press, 1955.

Deutsch, H. (1937), Absence of Grief. *Psychoanal. Quart.,* 6:12-22.

Eisendorfer, A. (1943), The Clinical Significance of the Single Parent Relationship in Women. *Psychoanal. Quart.,* 12:223-239.

Fenichel, O. (1945), The Concept of Trauma in Contemporary Psychoanalytic Theory. In: *Collected Papers,* II:49-69.

—— (1945), *The Psychoanalytic Theory of Neurosis.* New York: Norton.

Fraiberg, S. (1952), A Critical Neurosis in a Two-and-a-Half-Year-Old Girl. *The Psychoanalytic Study of the Child,* 7:173-215. New York: International Universities Press.

Freud, A. (1944), *Infants without Families.* New York: International Universities Press.

—— (1952), The Role of Bodily Illness in the Mental Life of Children. In: *Indications for Child Analysis. The Writings of Anna Freud,* Vol. IV. New York: International Universities Press, pp. 260-279.

—— (1960), Discussion of Dr. John Bowlby's paper, *The Psychoanalytic Study of the Child,* 15:53-62. New York: International Universities Press.

—— (1964), Comments on trauma. In: *The Writings of Anna Freud,* Vol. V. New York: International Universities Press, pp. 221-241.

—— (1965), *Normality and Pathology in Childhood. The Writings of Anna Freud, Vol. VI.* New York: International Universities Press.

—— & Burlingham, D. T. (1943), *War and Children*. New York: International Universities Press, 1944.

Freud, S. (1893), On the Psychical Mechanisms of Hysterical Phenomena. *Standard Edition*, 3:25-39. London: Hogarth Press, 1962.

—— (1895), Studies on Hysteria. *Standard Edition*, 2. London: Hogarth Press, 1955.

—— (1910), Leonardo da Vinci and a Memory of His Childhood. *Standard Edition*, 11:59-137. London: Hogarth Press, 1957.

—— (1913), Totem and Taboo. *Standard Edition*, 13:1-161. London: Hogarth Press, 1955.

—— (1916), Introductory Lectures on Psycho-Analysis, Lecture XVIII. *Standard Edition*, 16:273-285. London: Hogarth Press, 1963.

—— (1918), From the History of an Infantile Neurosis. *Standard Edition*, 17:3-122. London: Hogarth Press, 1955.

—— (1920), Beyond the Pleasure Principle. *Standard Edition*, 18:3-64. London: Hogarth Press, 1955.

—— (1923), The Ego and the Id. *Standard Edition*, 19:3-66. London: Hogarth Press, 1961.

—— (1926), Inhibitions, Symptoms and Anxiety. *Standard Edition*, 20:77-174. London: Hogarth Press, 1959.

Furman, R. A. (1964), Death of a Six-Year-Old's Mother During His Analysis. *The Psychoanalytic Study of the Child*, 19:377-397. New York: International Universities Press.

Greenacre, P. (1950), The Prepuberty Trauma in Girls. In: *Trauma, Growth, and Personality*. New York: International Universities Press, 1969, pp. 204-223.

—— (1952a), *Trauma, Growth and Personality*. New York: International Universities Press, 1969.

—— (1952b), Pregenital Patterning. *Internat. J. Psycho-Anal.*, 33:410-415.

—— (1953a), Penis Awe and Its Relation to Penis Envy. In: *Emotional Growth*, Vol. I. New York: International Universities Press, 1971, pp. 31-49.

—— (1953b), Certain Relationships between Fetishism and Faulty Development of the Body Image. In: *Emotional Growth*, Vol. I. New York: International Universities Press, 1971, pp. 9-30.

—— (1955), Further Considerations Regarding Fetishism. In: *Emotional Growth*, Vol. I. New York: International Universities Press, 1971, pp. 58-66.

—— (1956), Experiences of Awe in Childhood. In: *Emotional Growth*, Vol. I. New York: International Universities Press, 1971, pp. 67-92.

—— (1960), Further Notes on Fetishism. *The Psychoanalytic Study of the Child*, 15:191-207. New York: International Universities Press.

—— (1964), Infantile Trauma. Paper given at New York Psychoanalytic Society Meeting, June 9, 1964. Abstract: *Psychoanal. Quart.*, 34:148-150 (1965).

Hartmann, H. (1943), Problems of Infantile Neurosis. In: *Essays on Ego Psychology*. New York: International Universities Press, 1964, pp. 107-214.

—— (1958), Comments on the Scientific Aspects of Psychoanalysis. In: *Essays on Ego Psychology*. New York: International Universities Press, pp. 297-317.

—— Kris, E., & Loewenstein, R. M. (1951), Some Psychoanalytic Comments on "Culture and Personality." In: *Papers on Psychoanalytic Psychology* [*Psychological Issues, Monogr.* 14]. New York: International Universities Press, 1964, pp. 86-116.

Jessner, L., Blom, G. E., & Waldfogel, S. (1952), Emotional Implications of Tonsillectomy and Adenoidectomy in Children. *The Psychoanalytic Study of the Child*, 7:126-169. New York: International Universities Press.

—— & Kaplan, S. (1949), Emotional Reactions to Tonsillectomy and Adenoidectomy: preliminary survey. In: *Problems of Infancy and Childhood*. New York: Josiah Macy Foundation, pp. 97-118.

Jones, E. (1953), *The Life and Work of Sigmund Freud,* Vol. 1. New York: Basic Books.

Khan, M. R. (1963), The Concept of Cumulative Trauma. *The Psychoanalytic Study of the Child,* 18:286-306. New York: International Universities Press.

—— (1964), Ego Distortion, Cumulative Trauma, and the Role of Reconstruction in the Analytic Situation. *Internat. J. Psycho-Anal.,* 14:272-279.

Kris, E. (1956), The Recovery of Childhood Memories in Psychoanalysis. *The Psychoanalytic Study of the Child,* 11:54-88. New York: International Universities Press.

Kris, M. & Solnit, A. J. (1967), Trauma and Infantile Experiences: a Longitudinal Perspective. In: *Psychic Trauma,* Ed. S. Furst. New York: Basic Books, pp. 175-200.

Lipton, E. L. (1970), A Study of the Psychological Effects of Strabismus. *The Psychoanalytic Study of the Child,* 25:146-174. New York: International Universities Press.

Lussier, A. (1960), The Analysis of a Boy with a Congenital Deformity. *The Psychoanalytic Study of the Child,* 15:430-453. New York: International Universities Press.

Mahler, M. S. (1968), *On Human Symbiosis and the Vicissitudes of Individuation.* New York: International Universities Press.

Muensterberger, W. (1969), Psyche and Environment: Sociocultural Variations in Separation and Individuation. *Psychoanal. Quart.,* 38:191-216.

Meiss, M. L. (1952), The Oedipal Problem of a Fatherless Child. *The Psychoanalytic Study of the Child,* 7:216-229. New York: International Universities Press.

Murphy, W. F. (1958), Character, Trauma and Sensory Perception. *Internat. J. Psycho-Anal.,* 39:555-568.

—— (1959), Ego Integration, Trauma, and Insight. *Psychoanal. Quart.,* 28:514-532.

Neubauer, P. (1960), The One-Parent Child and His Oedipal Development. *The Psychoanalytic Study of the Child,* 15:286-309. New York: International Universities Press.

Niederland, W. G. (1961), The Problem of the Survivor, Part I: Some Remarks on the Psychiatric Evaluation of Emotional Disorders in Survivors of Nazi Persecution. *J. Hillside Hospital,* 10:233-247.

—— (1964), Psychiatric Disorders among Persecution Victims: A Contribution to the Understanding of Concentration Camp Pathology and Its After-Effects. *J. Nerv. and Mental Diseases,* 139:458-474.

—— & Krystal, H. (1965), Clinical Observations on the Survivor Syndrome. In: *Proceedings of the 121st Annual Meeting, American Psychiatric Association.* Washington, D. C., pp. 136-139.

Panel (1959), Psychological Consequences of Physical Illness in Childhood, V. Calef, reporter. *J. Amer. Psychoanal. Assn.,* 7:155-162.

Pearson, G. H. J. (1941), Effects of Operative Procedures on the Emotional Life of the Child. *Amer. J. Disease of Children,* 62:716.

Plank, E. & Horwood, C. (1961), Leg Amputation in a Four-Year-Old. *The Psychoanalytic Study of the Child,* 16:405-422. New York: International Universities Press.

Provence, S. & Lipton, R. (1962), *Infants in Institutions.* New York: International Universities Press.

Robertson, J. (1956), A Mother's Observation on the Tonsillectomy of Her Four-Year-Old Daughter: With Comments by Anna Freud. *The Psychoanalytic Study of the Child,* 11:410-436. New York: International Universities Press.

Roiphe, H. (1968), On an Early Genital Phase: With an Addendum on Genesis. *The Psychoanalytic Study of the Child*, 23:348-365. New York: International Universities Press.

Rosen, V. (1955), The Reconstruction of a Traumatic Childhood Event in a Case of Derealization. *J. Amer. Psychoanal. Assn.*, 3:211-221.

—— (1955), Strephosymbolia: An Intrasystemic Disturbance of the Synthetic Function of the Ego. *The Psychoanalytic Study of the Child*, 10:83-99. New York: International Universities Press.

Sandler, Joseph (1967), Trauma, Strain and Development. In: *Psychic Trauma,* ed. S. Furst. New York: Basic Books, pp. 154-174.

Schur, M. (1953), The Ego in Anxiety. In: *Drives, Affects, Behavior,* Vol. I, ed. R. M. Loewenstein. New York: International Universities Press, pp. 67-103.

Shambough, B. (1961), A Study of Loss Reactions in a Seven-Year-Old. *The Psychoanalytic Study of the Child*, 16:510-522. New York: International Universities Press.

Spitz, R. A. (1951), The Psychogenic Diseases in Infancy: An Attempt at Their Etiologic Classification. *The Psychoanalytic Study of the Child*, 6:255-275.

Waelder-Hall, J. (1946), Analysis of a Case of Night Terror. *The Psychoanalytic Study of the Child*, 2:189-228. New York: International Universities Press.

Waelder, R. (1965), Unpublished Contribution to Panel on The Concept of Trauma. Annual Meeting, American Psychoanalytic Association, May, 1965.

SYMBOLISM

JOHN DONADEO, M.D., *Reporter*

Participants: Drs. Charles Brenner (Chairman)—Renato J. Almansi
—Stuart S. Asch—John Donadeo—Vivian Fromberg—John Frosch—
Manuel Furer—Abe A. Goldman—Irving B. Harrison—Merl M. Jackel
—Edward D. Joseph—Henry F. Marasse—John B. McDevitt—Burness
E. Moore—William G. Niederland—Eugene V. Nininger—Lili L.
Peller (guest)—Joshua M. Perman—Morton F. Reiser—Arthur Root—
David L. Rubinfine—Joseph Schein—Herbert T. Schmale—Nathan P.
Segal—Tom G. Stauffer—Irving Sternschein.

INTRODUCTION

The study of the problem of symbolism concerns an area of
mental functioning which, though reaching at once to the heart
of both the theory and technique of psychoanalysis, has received
infrequent direct systematic treatment in our literature, although
it has occasionally figured secondarily in works devoted to the
explanation of other psychological problems and processes. This
relative neglect presents a strange paradox, inasmuch as from
the earliest years of psychoanalysis symbols were and have continued to be recognized as one of the irrefutable hallmarks of
unconscious mental activity. Freud said that he himself came only
slowly to a full recognition of their importance,[1] and not until
the fourth edition (1914) of *The Interpretation of Dreams* did he
devote a special section to the subject. In Lecture X of his *Introductory Lectures on Psychoanalysis* (1916), Freud's most im-

[1] ". . . I recognized the presence of symbolism in dreams from the very beginning. But it was only by degrees and as my experience increased that I arrived at a
full appreciation of its extent and significance . . ." (Freud, 1900, p. 350).

portant treatment of the subject of symbolism in dreams, he underscored its central position in psychoanalysis with the statement:
"Symbolism is perhaps the most remarkable chapter of the theory
of dreams" (p. 151).

The present report is based on the proceedings of a section of
the Kris Study Group of the New York Psychoanalytic Institute,
led by Dr. Charles Brenner, carried out in a series of seven
monthly meetings. While the study leans heavily on the work of
Ernest Jones, contained in his paper, "The Theory of Symbolism"
(1916)—the first direct, systematic exploration of symbolism in
the psychoanalytic literature—it ranges over other related data
from the psychoanalytic literature, illustrative case material from
the members' own day-to-day clinical work, as well as references
to some relevant findings from allied fields and disciplines.

The systematic approach to the study of symbolism began with
the need to establish a terminological base; the words "symbol"
and "symbolism" spring from deep roots in man's evolution, and
their meanings have expressed a wide variety of usages in proph-
ecy, wielding of power, language, religion, magic, play, and the
arts. Freud's great discoveries have made it possible to investigate
the deeper, unconscious sources and significance of symbols and
the processes which give rise to them, and to see them as integral
parts of man's psychological development.

DEFINITIONS

What precisely do we mean when we speak of symbols or of
symbolism? Webster's New International Dictionary (1947) de-
fines symbol as "That which stands for or suggests something else
by reason of relationship, association, convention, or accidental,
but not intentional resemblance. . . ." Is there a difference between the dictionary and the psychoanalytic definitions of symbols? This study represents one effort at an answer by a synthesis
of biological, developmental, and metapsychological approaches
to the phenomenon of symbolism in man.

Biological considerations of heredity, endowment, and maturational sequences and timetables are fundamental to any theory of
psychological development. Psychoanalysis assumes, for example,

that certain levels of biological maturation of the central and peripheral nervous systems (e.g., completion of myelinization of neural pathways) [2] are indispensable prerequisites for the psychic apparatus to register, organize, and deal with the primordial perceptual stimuli impinging on the organism from both internal and external sources. From a developmental point of view, any theory of symbols and their formation would require an explanation of the distinction between symbol formation and the formation of other differentiating components of psychological processes —conceptualizations, abstractions, cognitive acquisitions, and the like. This is so because symbols present ample evidence to suggest that experientially they constitute a unique category of indirect representations of unconscious mental activity, made up of complex ideational and affective elements. A metapsychological study of symbols must include the unfolding of the genetic, economic, and dynamic aspects of their content, as well as their characteristic attributes and functions in accordance with the topographic and structural viewpoints of psychoanalysis.

The development of theoretical propositions such as those outlined above can best be illustrated by the introduction of clinical data for their substantiation and further elaboration. A patient in analysis, on associating to a symptomatic act, produced memories and fantasies relating to masturbation which readily demonstrated that in the act involved his hand had "symbolized" his penis. Why had the substitution occurred, and what did it mean? Was this to be considered an instance of the psychoanalytic use of symbolism different from nonpsychoanalytic use and meaning of symbols? Recent research into ancient Sumerian cuneiform has shown that the earliest representations for man and woman unequivocally depicted the penis and the vagina, but during the course of subsequent millennia these symbols gradually underwent successive changes, until eventually they no longer resembled frank renderings of male and female genitalia. In contrast, repre-

---

[2] The transition from ape to *man* and the evolution within the *human family* itself show clearly the law of increasing differentiation and hierarchization. . . . As we know from the works of Flechsig, this development of the brain areas is paralleled in the ontogenetic development of man. This assumes that the time at which the connective fibers of the brain areas receive their sheath (myelinization) represents the beginning of the actual functioning of these areas (Werner, 1948, p. 49).

sentations of objects of "neutral" concern, such as those for cow and barley, remained relatively unchanged over the same long span of time. The transformation of the sexual symbols reflected a gradual replacement of a direct sexual expression, until finally the conventional symbol became an indirect disguised representation of an idea once clear and unequivocal.

This finding, centering directly on the role of evolving attitudes toward sexuality, highlights a particular significance of the substitution of hand for penis in the example cited and illustrates Jones's (1916) conclusions regarding symbol formation. He emphasized that symbols *always* defend against some idea or affect under repression and are therefore inaccessible to consciousness. Jones held firmly to the view that symbols are the outcome of intrapsychic conflict between repressing tendencies and the repressed contents. The most primary kind of symbolism is the equating of one part of the body with another, with one subsequently replacing the other. Further, the primary ideas of life are the only ones that can be symbolized, and they retain their importance in the unconscious throughout life. These ideas pertain to the bodily self, the family, birth, love, and death, and from them is derived the greatest part of the more secondary interests of the conscious mind. Energy flows *from* the primary ideas, never *to* them; and, because they constitute the most repressed part of the mind, it is understandable that symbolism can take place in *one* direction only: from the *concrete* to the *general* to the *abstract,* and never the other way around. For example, a steeple could symbolize the penis, but never a penis a steeple. Jones's argument represents the crucial basis for his differences with an important school of symbolism, whose most influential proponents at the time were Silberer[3] and Jung. This school held that "functional symbolism" arose from the need to express the abstract in terms of the concrete, which for Jones represented a confounding of two entirely different processes: metaphorical constructions and true symbolism. For Jones, the matter was one that could be resolved only by the full knowledge and acceptance of the role of unconscious forces. He maintained that experience invariably

---

[3] Silberer's "autosymbolic" phenomena and their relationship to alterations of consciousness approach some aspects of a hypothesis discussed later in this report.

showed that interpretation of symbols always stimulated the greatest repugnance and the greatest resistance to psychoanalytic work and hence was also at the center of the strongest opposition to psychoanalysis in general. These considerations, indeed, were what prompted Jones to undertake his special study of the phenomenon. His basic position is summed up in the statement that "only what is repressed is symbolized; only what is repressed *needs* to be symbolized" (p. 116).

Those who oppose ascribing to symbolism a primarily defensive function regard symbolism as too fundamental a characteristic of all mental life to be explained adequately from a single determining base. How, for instance, would a consciously and intentionally adopted use of a symbolic reference be explained on the basis of its value as a defense? A young man consciously intent on seducing a young woman he is taking home from a party said, as he put his car key into the lock, "I always carry my little key with me." Or, a chance observation of a little girl reciting playfully to a little boy, "You have a hot dog and I have a bun; let's get together and have some fun." In instances such as these, where the sexual reference was consciously clear and intentionally used, could the obvious symbolism be explained by Jones's criteria? These examples represent figures of speech in which the sexual references are used metaphorically; for in the stricter sense a symbol is not meant to be a communication but a product of unconscious processes, and its existence must be considered free of any communicative value. From a psychoanalytic point of view the two examples can and do also represent instances of true symbolism, for while expressing conscious wishes through metaphor, some unconscious content referable to forbidden infantile sexual strivings (preoedipal and oedipal fantasies and wishes, for example) would still be implicit and operative in them; that whatever conscious intent the use of the symbol was meant to convey, its formation was still rooted in forbidden and repressed strivings, and that the symbolic link, though used consciously in the present, had been unconsciously forged in the individual's distant past, i.e., in the earliest years and even months of life.

Insofar as the major argument against the primarily defensive function of symbols holds that symbols are so ubiquitous, so unique, so primordial an expression of mental functioning that they cannot be explained adequately as a defensive response, a more logical approach might be considered which attempts to enlarge the basis of their determining roots. Another formulation could be offered which, though still relying on the defensive aspects of symbolism, states that symbols represent a resolution of conflict by expressing both a wish and the defense against it (that symbols, like symptoms, always carry a forbidden idea disguised in such a way as to make it acceptable to the defending forces), but might at certain other times and under certain circumstances be determined by wholly conscious factors. Symbolism, similar in many respects to certain forms of regression—e.g., dreams, artistic activities, and play—may function "in the service of the ego." It could be postulated, then, that symbolism results less from reactions aimed at forestalling or resolving conflicts than from phenomena associated with unpleasant affects and requiring a mode of expression, as, for example, in the hot dog-bun rhyme related earlier, where affect could be released in a way comparable to that found in wit and humor. Or symbols could result, too, from the blocking of some need-tension such as in hunger, discomfort, pain, rather than wholly and directly from conflict—an argument fitting in quite readily with the concept that symbols may arise before repression or other defense mechanisms have been instituted. The content and implications of these tentative theoretical constructions leave little doubt that a wider, more general source than conflict and defense would be necessary for a satisfactory explanation of the complexity of factors involved in symbols and in symbolic processes. Accordingly, the implication of sources independent of conflict would represent not only a tenable but a necessary hypothesis to account for the role of symbolism in a widening spectrum of psychic activities, and one which appears to touch on multiple facets of instinctual and ego development, rather than a phenomenon related only to the ego's mechanisms of defense.

If we review briefly the characteristics of symbols and symbolism so far touched upon they seem to fall into three main groupings: (1) every symbol involves both instincts and defense; (2) the number of things symbolized are few and involve the basic interests of childhood, while objects for symbolization are almost infinite in number and variety; (3) symbol formation represents a particular type of mental functioning which, though discernible as a manifestation of conflict, yet may at the same time be present in many aspects of mental life outside of, and independent of, conflict.

In *The Interpretation of Dreams* (1900) Freud said, "Things that are symbolically connected today were probably united in prehistoric times by conceptual and linguistic identity. The symbolic relation seems to be a relic and a mark of former identity" (p. 352). In addition, Freud, noting that the patient's free associations frequently failed to elucidate symbolic elements in his dreams, suggested that symbols could be understood only as the result of our inherited knowledge of their significance. This view does not seem to correspond to what many psychoanalysts encounter in their clinical experience, where symbolic relationships are manifested in free association and are part of every analyst's daily psychoanalytic work. Psychoanalytic findings reflect unequivocally the individual instinctual and experiential sources of symbol formation.

Niederland, whose findings (1956, 1957), regarding water and river symbolism are well-known, has emphasized the regularity with which patients, in associating to a small body of water, refer to a sister or a "little mother." In addition, he cites examples from literary works which confirm the unconscious river/sister equation. Both Lord Byron and C. F. Meyer (a Swiss novelist and contemporary of Freud) had authenticated incestuous relations with their sisters. Niederland postulated on theoretical grounds that their writings were likely to contain demonstrable manifestations of such a relationship, most probably expressed in river symbolism. He found ample corroboration in Byron's *Childe Harold's Pilgrimage* (Canto III), composed for his half-sister Augusta, and in Meyer's *Die Richterin*, a novel replete with river symbolism. While collecting material from geographic and literary sources for his study on river symbolism, he came across an article entitled "The Rivers of Vicenza" by Antonio Barolini (1959), contemporary Italian poet and essayist. His attention was arrested by two passages in the essay in which the author had used the feminine gender in referring to a river, an unusual if not incorrect grammatical usage in Italian. He wrote the author, who was interested enough to reply, and said that he himself had been surprised when he found he had used the feminine gender for river. He *spontaneously* added that the essay had grown out of reminiscences of a long-dead sister and had, indeed, been written as a sort of memorial to her.

A brief clinical fragment will further demonstrate the thesis that early childhood experiences and individual reactions to them are the determining sources of symbolism. A depressed woman patient was dealing in her analysis with the effects on her of the birth of a younger sister. She dreamed of a blank white sheet of paper which she was "struggling to hold on to." Her associations expressed her rage at the younger sister's coming, together with references to food—especially to milk. Further associations led the analyst to identify the white piece of paper as the blank screen, the symbol for maternal breast (Lewin). She had lost the breast (mother) to her sister and, in the dream, had regained it and was struggling to hold on to it; she then added a verbal element from the dream: "It's mine." In another patient the dream screen was found to represent the state of satiation and bliss associated with possession of, or fusion with, the maternal breast.

These and other similar clinical findings have bolstered the disinclination to accept without qualification the classical view that symbols are permanent residues of early human history which remain constants in time and place and are carried on by a kind of Lamarckian inheritance. Such a premise leaves no room for the appearance of new symbols (occurring, for instance, with the invention of the Zeppelin) nor for the wide-ranging changeability of symbols within the same individual or among groups. Freud's earlier formulation of symbolism as a universal language could, however, be substantiated if the genetic emphasis were shifted from phylogenetic factors, difficult to prove in any case from our present knowledge, to demonstrable, concrete, and essentially sensory determinants arising in the course of individual human development.

FORMATION OF SYMBOLS

The emphasis on the vicissitudes of individual development brings into sharp focus the importance of establishing some clear distinction between the process of forming symbols and the development of other forms of indirect psychic representations. Psychoanalysis has as yet not provided an adequate set of criteria for making a satisfactory distinction. Any information gathered from unraveling the constituents of symbol formation or the unique characteristics of symbols could perhaps lead to clues as to when symbols first appear in mental life, and hopefully throw some light on those unique features which set symbols apart from all other mental products. Any effort at examining in detail the characteristic components and qualities of symbols would have to begin with the identification and elucidation of prerequisites and precursors of symbol formation.

How, then, approach the task of identifying the "raw materials," the determining internal and external experiences and events that appear traceable in symbols and in the processes of their formation? First among the so-called "raw materials," it seems plausible to assume, are memory traces of perceptions and registrations of stimuli impinging on the psychic apparatus from all the sensory pathways. The visual, auditory, tactile, kinesthetic, and proprioceptive phenomena, linked with, from the point of view of drive theory, an indispensable concomitant, experiences of gratification and/or frustration, would together warrant consideration as not only the model for, but also the irreducible elements in symbol formation. There can be little argument that symbols are perceptual in character, vividly so, as attested by their concrete, frequently pictorial, primary-process quality. These primordial formations may indeed represent the already unfolding symbolic process, but such primitive experiences may be merely the precursors—necessary prerequisites—but would not yet qualify as symbols. What is precursor and what symbol, and when and how does the transformation take place? It is tempting to view the hallucinatory wish fulfillment of earliest infancy, with its gratification/frustration interplay, its attempt at establishing a perceptual identity, its capacity for making discharge of tension possible, already a true symbol, an expression of nascent symbolic functioning. In his paper "The Breast-Face Equation" (1960), Almansi reached the conclusion, on the basis of clinical, archeological, and other evidence, that the eyes may symbolize the nipples. He postulated that in the very young infant there is a "primitive perceptual cluster" made up of the sensation of the nipple in the mouth and the concurrent vision of the mother's face. To this he added that, according to Spitz (1957) ". . . at about the age of three months when the child is deprived of the nipple, its eyes deviate from the mother's face in the general direction of the breasts, thus leading to the superimposition of these two percepts, which then become fused, and [also] it is at this age level that the aggressive drive comes to the fore as a consequence of the repeated frustration experienced at the breast." Almansi suggested that the face-breast or eye-nipple equation may constitute the first instance of symbolism and indeed be the model for all later symbol formation. He emphasized the role of frustration and the vicissitudes of aggression in symbol formation.

One may cite here an instance of symbol formation at an early stage of development. A three-and-a-half-year-old boy, after having had playful contact with his pregnant mother's fluctuant abdomen, reported a succession of water dreams with abundant and persistent production of fantasies rich in water-birth symbolism. Such phenomena occurring at age three and a half years may have drawn upon symbolic formations from much earlier water experiences, such as being placed into and lifted out of water by the mother during bathing.

The problem may be explored further by asking whether the transitional object qualifies as a true symbol, or is an example of a precursor for the later establishment of symbols for mother. Here caution must be exercised against deriving facile conclusions from broad assumptions and speculations connected with observations of infant behavior. Any specific claims for very early responses must be measured against the global and indiscriminate way infants experience and respond to all stimuli; it is essential to keep in mind that adequate development and maturation of spinal tracts is a necessary condition for the conduction of proprioceptive stimuli and for them to become meaningful. In essence, it may be assumed that while early experiences may well influence later symbol formation, these early experiences are continuously being filtered through a progressively developing and maturing ego.

What is the influence of developmental factors on symbolism, and how do developmental sequences influence symbol formation? Can it be assumed that the specific characteristics of the various stages of ego development bear any relation to the striking difference between the number of sexual symbols and other symbols, and also to the many meanings and uses of sexual symbols? Is there a phase-specific sequence discernible in symbolism, and, if so, would it be valid to postulate a hierarchy of symbols, paralleling a growing sophistication and increasing capacity for abstraction, from the most primitive primary process ideation to the most abstract forms of representation? Clinical experience reveals, for instance, a multitude of symbolic representations of the phallus. The spear, the Empire State Building, or a Zeppelin are all symbols for the phallus, but they are in certain respects quite different from one another. The phallic attributes of sadistic penetration, awesome size, or distension and soaring are separate and distinct attributes, and while they all denote phallic content, may not each be related and traceable to given specific levels of psychosexual development? Could not each one then express the outcome of some specific conflict arising at a particular point in development? Phallic symbols with explosive attributes, those from which water flows, those capable of elongation, those denoting the evil phallus (e.g., the devil, snakes), all could have similar specificity regarding level of development and content of the conflict. Further, one might argue, these variable secondary attributes may represent an important distinguishing characteristic of sexual symbols, depicting a more direct, primary process formation originating from and rooted in the vividly sensorial early experiences. In contrast, nonsexual symbols seem to possess relatively little secondary variability, involve a much greater sophistication, and hence reflect a somewhat later development indicative of a maturer ego dealing with a more circumscribed conflict. Examples of these latter symbols would include royalty or rulers as symbols for parents, vermin for siblings, and so forth.

The hypotheses and formulations so far developed pertaining

to the characteristics of symbols, their forerunners, their ultimate somatic sources, and the above attempt at classification, while they may substantially aid in clarifying and establishing some aspects of the essential features of symbols, do not set them apart from other derivatives of unconscious contents and processes; no unifying concepts of symbolism seem to be contained in them. The characteristics so far attributed to symbols, such as primary process, reactions to somatic sensations, their potentials for defense, and so forth, do not constitute sufficiently specific criteria, singly or in combination, for these criteria could be applied as well to the other derivatives of the unconscious, such as concept formation, fantasy formation, the establishment of body and ego boundaries, the development of object relations and object constancy, the differentiation of the self, and many others, as well as to symbolism itself.

Can the broadening scope of autonomy of ego functions include the process of symbolization as one of the autonomous functions of the ego which, in conjunction with the concomitant and/or subsequent development of other ego functions and capacities, accounts for the formation of symbols? The formation of symbols in the service of defensive needs and pressures might occur only after repression, denial, and displacement, as well as other defense mechanisms have been instituted. At the same time, symbols might serve other developmental and maturational requirements apart from defense, such as the acquisition of major skills and controls, reality testing, and the acquisition of speech and language. If symbolization proceeded as an autonomous ego activity, no matter what aspect of development it served, the process of symbol formation itself would still be unique and stand apart from all other unconscious mental processes and their derivatives. Ascribing autonomy to the symbolic function does not, of course, necessarily afford any clearer explanation of the phenomenon. More than the usual psychoanalytic amplification of the nature of the process seems to be required, and an examination of symbols as described, defined, and explained by workers in other disciplines, especially by anthropologists, might be useful.

ANTHROPOLOGY AND SYMBOLISM

Three representative anthropological papers (White, 1940, 1942; Sahlins, 1949), which attempt to explain the symbol and how, in the anthropologist's terms, it has been related to the beginnings of human culture, were discussed by the group. White's general thesis may be expressed as follows: All human behavior originates in the use of symbols; it was the symbol that transformed anthropoids into men; it is the symbol that transforms the infant of *homo sapiens* into a human being; human behavior is symbolic behavior, and the symbol is "the universe of humanity." White maintains that the essential qualitative difference between animals and humans in what he calls the "capacity for symbolling"; this capacity indicates a complete difference in quality, not one of degree, between the mentality of anthropoids and humans. Animals do not and cannot enter and participate in the world the human being experiences and in which he lives.

White acknowledges that primates are able to use tools, even with delicacy rather than with mere strength, and among the higher apes, even in a conceptual way. Here, "conceptual" implies the formation of a configuration of behavior in which animal, tool, and the thing upon which the tool is to be used are functionally related to one another. But it was the introduction of word symbols for tools—axe, knife, hammer, etc.—that transformed anthropoid tool-behavior into human tool-behavior. The symbol, particularly in word form, provides the element of continuity in man's tool-behavior and experience, resulting in a "progressive accumulation" which over time constitutes culture.

According to Sahlins, the similarities between subhuman and human societies are very slight. There exist between the species both a process of generic continuity and of specific discontinuity. The social behavior of primates is the foundation of some of the general features of human society; however, no specific trait of cultural society is a direct survival of some specific trait of primate social behavior. This discontinuity is due to the fact that subhuman primate society is a direct expression of the physiology of the species, whereas cultural traits govern the social adaptation of the human primate, and are based on symbol values and the process of symbolling. Sahlins summarizes the most significant advances in the early evolution of cultural behavior as: (1) the division of labor by sex and the establishment of the family on this basis; (2) the invention of kinship; (3) the incest prohibition and its extension through exogamy, thus extending kinship; (4) the overcoming of primate competition over food in favor of sharing and cooperation; and (5) the abolition of other primate conflicts leading to the establishment of dominance hierarchies. These advances are complementary, and, whatever their order of appearance or relative significance, together they constitute the great triumphs of early culture, the social counterparts of the continuous tool activity that enabled man to become the dominant life form.

Though admittedly cursory, this sampling of views of representative anthropological workers leaves little doubt about the overriding importance attributed by them to the role of symbolic processes in man's evolution; indeed, the capacity for symbolization stands as the crucial differentiating feature which separated man from all lower forms of life. However, any attempt to correlate the concept of "symbolling" as used in anthropology with symbolism as used in psychoanalysis must be approached warily by psychoanalysts. Disagreement rests chiefly on the inadequacy and, to some extent, the superficiality of anthropological explanations; any attempts at establishing phylogenetic links between symbolling in subhuman species and the development of symbol formation in man cannot be fruitful for psychoanalytic requirements unless they encompass those factors which are fundamental to the science of psychoanalysis, namely, the metapsychological conceptualizations which form its framework. For instance, no matter whatever else enters into symbol formation, it seems incontrovertible that anxiety and defense do constitute critical components of it. The psychoanalytic view of the boy fantasying the image of a girl with a penis first of all presupposes that the boy has already perceived the difference between the sexes. Secondly, as a result of anxiety, there comes into play not only the the defense mechanism of denial but, beyond this, a process which demonstrates a basic precondition of symbol formation—namely, the need to deny the painful perception of difference, to substitute a perceptual identity, and to bring about a reduction in the painful effects of conflict. For psychoanalysts, such an example may be paradigmatic and constitutes the strongest of arguments to show that the concept of symbolism as used in psychoanalysis is not the same as that referred to in other disciplines.

It has often been postulated that the development of the capacity for speech and language ushered in the use of symbols. To many, the preverbal experiences the infant and child accumulate from the relationships with their immediate objects and environment, encompassing both conscious and unconscious contents seem even more important. Does the human infant at birth already possess the capacity for symbolism? If not, at what point does symbolism occur, i.e., at which point has the symbol been invested with the ability to relate to something that stands for something else? Does this capacity for symbolism in the human infant differ from the symbolling in animals? Animal symbolling denotes the perception of relationship between two objects, but this relationship remains bound to and dependent on physical and intrinsic qualities; the response is stereotyped. It repeats an event experienced in the past without evolving beyond this point, and does not lead to the generation and perception of new relationships. Man, on the contrary, assumes an active role in the symbolization process; he ascribes meanings to relationships between phenomena occurring in the experiential sphere which make possible an increasingly expanding complementarity of new meanings and new relationships, and this underscores the genuinely creative nature of symbolism in man. The advent of this capacity was momentous in man's development, for it determined his evolutionary course and set him apart from, and eventually above, all other forms with which he had up to that point shared common origins and a common development. The human infant, already possessing this creative capacity from birth, either actual or potential, is thus from birth distinctly different from all other primates. While there may be only small differences between man and other primates in their potential capacities for speech, use of tools, learning of tasks, etc., the capacity to form and use symbols in this creative sense is a uniquely human attribute with no direct parallel demonstrable in subhuman species. This characteristic, which so effectively distinguishes the human individual, has produced profound effects on the development of the human community, for the transmission of these creatively symbolic contents to successive generations has fashioned the complex external and internal edifices of human history and culture.

From phylogenetic factors in the development of symbolism, our study shifts to consideration of a more specific psychoanalytic and ontogenetic nature, especially to the role of ego development and its relation to the symbolic process. The ego must be sufficiently developed to the point of having acquired some rudimentary capacity to differentiate between the object to be symbolized and the symbol. Though not precisely fixed as to time and extent, elements of drive, anxiety, and defense are also intimately involved in the establishment of this relationship. The hallucinatory wish fulfillment might, in this sense, be considered to satisfy these requirements for symbolization. A clear distinction, however, may be drawn between the hallucinated wish fulfillment and a true symbol. The hallucinated fulfillment stands among the earliest responses of the primitive psychic apparatus to the peremptoriness of instinctual demands, bringing about an immediate discharge of accumulated tension. Symbols, on the other hand, represent the response of a more highly differentiated psychic organization to an instinctual pressure, a response which makes possible both a partial discharge of tension as well as a delay in its discharge and a postponement of gratification until appropriate conditions in reality can be found, or reality altered, in order to achieve it.

To pursue this thesis, the postponement of a gratification, in the sense of anticipating it, presupposes the presence of some notion of the concept of "future," so that symbol formation and concept formation might share some similar sources and mutual interdependence. Caution dictates against the possible blurring of distinctions between the development of concepts and the formation of symbols; while both processes may share a common source, they need not be the same. For example, the perception of movement in his own body may be the ultimate source of the infant's concept of the use of movable objects, like a bicycle, and also for the symbolic meaning of falling in the case of a phobia of heights. Each derivative, however, follows its own course of development to a different end point. Difficulty in distinguishing between the processes of symbolization and concept formation are readily apparent in these questions. If a hungry, crying infant stops crying when the mother enters the room and before she feeds him, does this signify that the mother is now a symbol, or is this a manifestation of concept formation? Or, is the blanket a somewhat older child clings to and rubs a symbol for the mother? While these questions relate to the issue of differentiating symbol and concept formation, they are actually a part of the larger problem raised earlier in this discussion, namely, are symbols different from all other forms of psychic representations? Symbols do stand apart and are a unique phenomenon, different from all others in mental life; it seems likely that they also are unique as to genesis, development, and functions.

It is tempting to explain the special qualities of symbols by ascribing them "functions," but this comes uncomfortably close to teleological reasoning, however valid the statements might be on a descriptive level. For instance, the statement that symbols "have more to do with feelings than with logical thought" implies that a major function of symbolism is the regulating of affects. Such a view is demonstrated by Suzanne Langer's (1942) claim that the literature insufficiently emphasizes that function of symbolization which attempts to formulate experience as imaginable. This was expressed by her contention that in the newborn there is a "pressure or demand" from the material of perception to be represented in the psyche, and that symbols arise as the consequence of such perceptual phenomena's linking up with drive tensions, so that discharge may be effected according to the primary-process principles. The role of symbol formation in the organization of these mental representations of perceptions and drive phenomena was discussed by Donadeo (see Panel, 1961) and will not be elaborated here.

REGRESSION AND SYMBOL FORMATION

A hypothetical construction offered by Rubinfine (see Panel, 1961) takes up the role of alterations of consciousness and of

regression in symbolization. Prefacing his argument with a statement from *The Interpretation of Dreams*,[4] in which Freud (1900)
discussed some characteristics of the state of consciousness necessary for the pursuit of dream interpretation, Rubinfine postulated
that a reduction in sensory stimulation of sufficient degree to
interfere with the perception and testing of reality produces a
regressed ego state, including an alteration of consciousness. In
such a state, boundaries or barriers which differentiate self from
nonself become fluid, and "imaging" replaces perception. One of
the possible issues of this "state" is the formation of symbols.
Rubinfine found concurrence for this formulation in Isakower's
(1938) study of experiences attendant on falling asleep,[5] and from
experiments (Bexton et al., 1954) wherein sensory deprivation
led to hallucinatory phenomena ranging from simple geometric
patterns to fully formed hallucinations described as "dreams with
your eyes open."

From these experiments, in which stimuli impinging on all
sensory modalities—tactile and kinesthetic as well as visual and
auditory—were kept at minimal or zero levels, it was inferred
that ego structure and functions such as defense, reality testing,
and perception, require a constant and continually varied sensory
input from the external environment to maintain their stability.
Regressed ego states, as shown in these experiments, favor the
development of "imagery," and these images constitute the "raw
material" of symbolism. When such images are subjected to
primary process mental functioning, symbol formation results (see
Panel, 1961). Thus, the significant factor in symbol formation is
the ego state involved, and because altered ego states are universal,
symbols—as products of these altered states—share in this univer-
sality and so develop independently of individual life experiences.

The breast-face equation, referred to above, may be an instance

---

[4] ". . . What is in question, evidently, is the establishment of a psychical state
which, in its distribution of psychical energy (that is, of mobile attention), bears
some analogy to the state before falling asleep—and no doubt also to hypnosis. As
we fall asleep, 'involuntary ideas' emerge. . . . As the involuntary ideas emerge
they change into visual and acoustic images" (Freud, 1900, p. 102).

[5] Isakower notes that when cathexis of the "side of the perceptual system which
faces outwards is relatively depleted, while the side which faces towards the ego is
more abundantly cathected . . . [there results a] regressive diminution of differentiation" (1938, pp. 337-338).

of this hypothetical development to the extent that it occurs at a time when ego boundaries are still in a fluctuating state, thus implying an "archaic ego state" which favors symbol formation. In addition, the formulation suggests a link between denial and sensory deprivation in which denial sets the conditions for symbol formation as the representation for the denied percept: indeed, the symbol could be seen as a response to "perception hunger." The hypothesis, however, does not explain the common use of symbols by individuals who show neither a global regression nor even the specific regression of blurring of ego boundaries or of perception. For example, in the "key-penis" example cited earlier, the consciously determined use of the symbol "key" for a seductive communication did not presume or seem to reflect such a regressed state. The dilemma involved might be outlined as follows:

Rubinfine's hypothesis supposes a regression to an ego state where the differences between "key" and "penis" are minimized and the identification between them is made by primitive means (primary processes). But did this "sophisticated communication" require such a blurring of ego boundaries, or even a perceptual deprivation, in order to be formed and expressed? And furthermore, did the girl who, after all, must have understood the inference, first have to have experienced some blurring of *her* ego boundaries? Of course, this argument, because it depicts, not an instance of sensory deprivation, but one of sensory selection shared in by the girl, does not necessarily invalidate the hypothesis.

If symbols do occur as replacements or substitutes for denied percepts, then we are faced with only another instance of a return of the repressed. If this is so, it leaves unexplained how symbols differ from other derivatives of the unconscious. One answer may be that while repression deals with all kinds of content—affects, memories, drives, conflicts, etc.—symbolism is a *special* response because it deals with perceptual data only. Despite this argument's appeal, it cannot be conclusively demonstrated that symbol formation is restricted to regressed ego states. On empirical grounds, such a restriction would seem not to do justice to the richness and breadth of symbolic functioning in mental life in all its aspects, an argument identical to the one raised earlier against symbol formation as a defensive mechanism. Symbolism can and does take place in nonregressed ego states with normal consciousness.

In support of the thesis that sensory deprivation may stimulate symbolism, the work of Fisher and Paul (1959) presents clear evidence for the impact of primary process reasoning on "images" and dreams obtained from exposing subjects to tachistoscopically presented subliminal stimuli,[6] with the subjects in a state of "reduced self-awareness." In considering the relevance of these observations, however, a terminological difficulty presents itself regarding the precise meaning of "image" and "imaging" in the basic hypothesis. Is there a point at which an image becomes a symbol? In the paper cited, no distinction is made, either, between images and day residues, for example, nor is it explained how symbols are derived from these "images." When one turns to the question of what occurs in an analytic hour, it is debatable whether the appearance of illusory visual phenomena warrants broad conclusions regarding either regressive alterations in the cathexis of the perceptual apparatus or in states of consciousness and symbolic processes. A symbol may be alluded to or reported by a patient during an analytic session, e.g., when a dream is recounted. Nevertheless, as in the case of any other registration, because a symbol is laid down structurally as a memory trace, under appropriate conditions it may be recalled in a state of full consciousness. A day residue percept might be subjected to primary processes, something which might occur even at the moment of registration, but this is not synonymous with symbol formation. And, certainly, not all imagery is symbolic. Whether a symbol appears or not would depend on the degree of drive cathexis with which the imagery is invested and on the presence and intensity of conflict. Without such prerequisites, other phenomena, such as, for example, eidetic imagery, may become manifest.

Objections also can be raised to the gross comparison of phenomena associated with a supposed structural regression and the ego state of the infant. There is obviously a major difference

[6] Fisher and Paul found that the post-exposure "images" showed transformations and distortions of the stimulus and that the stimulus also emerged in the manifest content of subsequent dreams.

between the infant and the older child and adult, for after infancy a multitude of maturational and developmental as well as experiential phenomena have accumulated and have been organized and established. In sum, no case for causality or specificity can be made concerning imagery and symbol formation that is related to sensory deprivation, regressed ego states, or altered states of consciousness.

An alternate proposal can be suggested, in which exactly opposite conditions—namely, a marked increase in sensory stimulation —can be thought of as favoring symbol formation. The stimulation could have its source in the external environment, as well as in heightened instinctual drive activity, augmented, of course, by those perceptions which engender or intensify conflict. Nonetheless, there is the paradoxical possibility that overstimulation, acting as a "perceptual shock," might mobilize defenses to such a degree that sensory deprivation could ensue and thus lead to the formation of symbols on the basis of the aforementioned "perceptual hunger." It can even be argued that hyperstimulation can lead to a "shutting down" of the perceptual apparatus, typified at extreme limits, perhaps, by syncope.

SYMBOLS AND THE OEDIPAL PHASE

The final arguments presented in this study deal with two themes relating to particular determinants and functions of symbols. The flowering of symbolism in early oedipal children indicates that there is much to support the proposition that *true* symbol formation coincides with the oedipal period and serves as a defense against oedipal stress. Inasmuch as the child is neither able to discharge his sexual and aggressive drive tensions upon his primary objects, nor run away, symbol formation is the compromise (e.g., when a child dreams of King and Queen). In addition, symbols also appear prominently in the child's play during this period.

The burgeoning of symbolism in the oedipal phase, which seems to occur in children of every culture, demonstrates the symbol's capacity for effecting reductions of the intense inner conflicts the child experiences from the increase in genital excitement that he is neither biologically nor psychologically ready to discharge fully. The wave of sexual excitement (and aggression) that cannot reach its aim flows into collateral channels, bringing about a complex array of imagery, fantasy, and imaginative play. Symbolism links huge portions of outer and inner experiences to bodily functions, body parts, and feelings, making the multitudinous impingements of stimuli and percepts familiar and manageable through organizing, integrating, and synthesizing them. It thus simultaneously serves the claims of all three mental institutions, the id, ego, and superego, according to the principle of multiple function (Waelder, 1936). Other mammals when reaching genitality can discharge their sexual drives fully, external conditions permitting. Only the human child can erect inner barriers against the aims of the instinctual drives. And only human beings use symbols. Even more than the use of tools, the use of symbols is distinctly human. Rather than stating that man has created symbols, it could perhaps be said that man himself has been created by the capacity to form symbols.

A final hypothesis would classify symbols as a compromise formation and would include symbolism among the restitutional phenomena aimed at preserving and/or recovering lost objects. The symbolic function, so pervasive in severely ill schizophrenics, may represent this aspect of symbolism in its most demonstrable form. Caution, however, should deter us from extrapolating from severe psychopathology to normal developmental phenomena. There is a wide difference, it must be emphasized, between the normal functioning of an infant's and child's mind and the "breakdown products" of psychosis (Glover, 1950).

This report presents the salient arguments that emerged from our series of discussions on symbolism. Neither the report nor the summary that concludes it adheres strictly to a formal, chronological order of the ideas, opinions, and arguments expressed. In the interests of avoiding repetition and redundancy, some selection and organization of the material has been made. The report does, however, follow the broad general sequence in which the major themes were introduced and developed in the course of the study. What has been sacrificed by not reporting the arguments in literal sequence and detail, it is hoped, will have been compensated for by a greater coherence and clarity.

Of course, no report could fully convey the lively nature of the discussions themselves, which were characterized throughout by the unflagging interest and enthusiasm of every member of the group as they searched for a deeper and wider knowledge of this fundamental yet elusive phenomenon of man's mental life. Nor can this report adequately portray the devotion and skill brought to all aspects of the discussion by Dr. Charles Brenner who, as leader and moderator, guided the study smoothly through all of its phases.

This study group, a numerically limited forum for the exchange of ideas and experiences in an informal setting, continues the tradition established by its founder. Ernst Kris originally brought to these study groups the glowing qualities of zest, humor, and kindness, all of which suffused his profound knowledge and understanding of psychoanalysis. Of his many gifts, that of inspired and inspiring teacher was not the least.

SUMMARY

Definitions

Distinctions were drawn between the psychoanalytic and the nonpsychoanalytic meaning of the term symbol, including its usage not only in the general dictionary sense, but also as defined in other disciplines, especially comparative psychology and anthropology.

A "true symbol" in psychoanalytic terms would include its unconscious sources and the metapsychological principles which govern its development.

Several distinctions were suggested between symbols and other forms of indirect representation, such as simile, metaphor, conceptualization, etc.

Characteristics of Symbols

Symbols are vividly sensorial phenomena arising from all perceptual modalities. The flow of energy in their formulation follows one direction only: from the concrete to the general to the abstract; never the other way around.

Symbols have a strong affective charge derived from their unconscious and instinctual sources, and present intense resistance against becoming conscious. Freud maintained that it was not possible to associate to them, and he suggested that knowledge of them was independent of the individual's life experiences. This view, however, does not correspond to the experience of many psychoanalysts in their clinical work in which there are repetitive and unequivocal evidences of the individual instinctual and experiential sources of symbol formation.

The number of symbols is virtually limitless, the things symbolized very few. These involve the instinctual interests of the infant and child: the drives and their objects—namely, the body, its parts and functions, parents, siblings, the family, love, and death.

Prerequisites, Precursors, and Conditions Necessary for Symbol Formation

Beginning with memory traces of sensations, objects, and experiences of frustration and/or gratification, the process may be said to include the blocking of need tensions, the advent of conflict, the institution of repression, regressions in the perceptual sphere and alterations of consciousness, sensory deprivations as well as overstimulation of the sensory apparatus and the concomitant development of ego functions. No direct or continuous line of development exists between symbolism in man and the "symbolling" activities in subhuman species.

Ego Development and Symbol Formation

Symbolism was viewed as a process spanning the full range of developing ego structures and functions, from rudiments of organization of perceptions in earliest life to the highest levels of abstraction and secondary processes. In this sense it could be considered a continuum, with symbols acquiring ever new and different additional meanings at each succeeding stage and level of development.

Little support appears for considering symbolism an autonomous function, either in a phylogenetic or ontogenetic frame of reference. It seems to be a form of mental activity close to instinctual and drive phenomena in character, contributing to all aspects of ego development from the earliest primitive organizations of psychogenesis to the ultimate elaboration of personality and character.

The Multiple Functions of Symbolism

Symbolism links multitudinous sensory phenomena from the external world to bodily functions, feelings, and body parts and relates these to objects and experiences of gratification and/or frustration, making them familiar and integrated through ordering and organizing them. It thus serves all three psychic institutions through all phases of development. The defensive potential particularly proliferates during the oedipal phase.

Symbols, in the psychoanalytic sense, do not have a primary communicative function, and, though communication is a later linguistic derivative, symbols are not designed to communicate the unconscious component of the symbol, but rather result in the opposite. This is perhaps most clearly observed in the service of defense, where symbolism provides collateral channels for the discharge of sexual and aggressive drives, thus deflecting and inhibiting them and/or offering substitutes for the primary objects and aims.

BIBLIOGRAPHY

Almansi, R. J. (1960), The Breast-Face Equation. *J. Amer. Psychoanal. Assn.*, 8:43-70.
Barolini, A. (1959), The Rivers of Vicenza. *The Reporter*, May 1.
Bexton, W. H., Heron, W. & Scott, T. H. (1954), Effects of Decreased Variation in the Sensory Environment. *Canad. J. Psychol.*, 8:70-76.
Blank, H. R. (1958), Dreams of the Blind. *Psychoanal. Quart.*, 27:158-174.
Brenner, C. (1955), *An Elementary Textbook of Psychoanalysis*. New York: International Universities Press.
Fisher, C. & Paul, I. H. (1959), The Effect of Subliminal Visual Stimulation on Images and Dreams: A Validation Study. *J. Amer. Psychoanal. Assn.*, 7:35-83.
Freud, S. (1900), The Interpretation of Dreams. *Standard Edition*, 4 & 5. London: Hogarth Press, 1953.
—— (1910), The Antithetical Meaning of Primal Words. *Standard Edition*, 11:153-162. London: Hogarth Press, 1957.

—— (1916), Introductory Lectures on Psycho-Analysis (Chapter X). *Standard Edition,* 15:149-169. London: Hogarth Press, 1963.

Glover, E. (1950), Functional Aspects of the Mental Apparatus. In: *On the Early Development of Mind.* New York: International Universities Press, 1956, pp. 364-378.

Isakower, O. (1938), A Contribution to the Pathopsychology of Phenomena Associated with Falling Asleep. *Internat. J. Psycho-Anal.,* 19:331-345.

Jones, E. (1916), The Theory of Symbolism. In: *Papers on Psycho-Analysis.* Boston: Beacon Press, 1961, pp. 87-144.

Kubie, L. (1953), The Distortion of the Symbolic Process in Neurosis and Psychosis. *J. Amer. Psychoanal. Assn.,* 1:59-85.

Langer, S. K. (1942), *Philosophy in a New Key: A Study in the Symbolism of Reason, Rite and Art.* Cambridge: Harvard University Press, 1960.

Lewin, B. D. (1950), *The Psychoanalysis of Elation.* New York: Norton.

Niederland, W. G. (1956), River Symbolism, Part I. *Psychoanal. Quart.,* 25:464-504.

—— (1957), River Symbolism, Part II. *Psychoanal. Quart.,* 26:50-75.

Panel (1961), The Psychoanalytic Theory of the Symbolic Process, N. P. Segel, reporter. *Journal of the American Psychoanalytic Association,* 9:146-157.

Rycroft, C. (1956), Symbolism and the Primary and Secondary Processes. *Internat. J. Psycho-Anal.,* 37:137-146.

Sahlins, M.D. (1959), The Social Life of Monkeys, Apes and Primitive Men. In: *Readings in Anthropology,* Vol. II, ed. by Morton H. Fried. New York: Crowell.

Sharpe, E. (1940), Psycho-Physical Problems Revealed in Language: An Examination of Metaphor. *Internat. J. Psycho-Anal.,* 21:201-213.

Silberer, H. (1909), Report on a Method of Eliciting and Observing Certain Symbolic Hallucination-Phenomena. In: D. Rapaport, *The Organization and Pathology of Thought.* New York: Columbia University Press, 1951, pp. 195-207.

—— (1912), On Symbol-Formation. In: D. Rapaport, *The Organization and Pathology of Thought.* New York: Columbia University Press, 1951, pp. 208-233.

Spitz, R. A. (1957), *No and Yes.* New York: International Universities Press.

Waelder, R. (1936), The Principle of Multiple Function. *Psychoanal. Quart.,* 5:45-62.

Webster's New International Dictionary (1947), Second Edition, Springfield, Mass., G. & C. Merriam Co.

Werner, H. (1948), *Comparative Psychology of Mental Development.* New York: International Universities Press.

White, L. A. (1940), The Symbol: The Origin and Basis of Human Behavior. In: *The Science of Culture: A Study of Man and Civilization.* New York: Grove Press, 1949, pp. 22-39.

—— (1942), On the Use of Tools by Primates. In: *The Science of Culture: A Study of Man and Civilization.* New York: Grove Press, 1959, pp. 40-49.